Student Applications Book

Great Source Education Group
a Houghton Mifflin Company
Wilmington, Massachusetts

www.greatsource.com

AUTHORS

Laura Robb
Author

Powhatan School, Boyce, Virginia
Laura Robb, author of *Reading Strategies That Work* and *Teaching Reading in Middle School*, has taught language arts at Powhatan School in Boyce, Virginia, for more than 30 years. She is a co-author of the *Reading and Writing Sourcebooks* for grades 3–5 and the *Summer Success: Reading* program. Robb also mentors and coaches teachers in Virginia public schools and speaks at conferences throughout the country on reading and writing.

Ron Klemp
Contributing Author

Los Angeles Unified School District, Los Angeles, California
Ron Klemp is the Coordinator of Reading for the Los Angeles Unified School District. He has taught Reading, English, and Social Studies and was a middle school Dean of Discipline. He is also coordinator/facilitator at the Secondary Practitioner Center, a professional development program in the Los Angeles Unified School District. He has been teaching at California State University, Cal Lutheran University, and National University.

Wendell Schwartz
Contributing Author

Adlai Stevenson High School, Lincolnshire, Illinois
Wendell Schwartz has been a teacher of English for 36 years. For the last 24 years he also has served as the Director of Communication Arts at Adlai Stevenson High School. He has taught gifted middle school students for the last 12 years, as well as teaching graduate-level courses for National-Louis University in Evanston, Illinois.

Editorial:
Design:
Illustrations:

Developed by Nieman, Inc.
Ronan Design: Christine Ronan, Sean O'Neill, Maria Mariottini
Mike McConnell

Printed in the United States of America

International Standard Book Number: 0–669–48861–5
(Student Applications Book)

2 3 4 5 6 7 8 9 – RRDC – 08 07 06 05 04 03

International Standard Book Number: 0–669–49082–2
(Student Applications Book, Teacher's Edition)

2 3 4 5 6 7 8 9 – RRDC – 08 07 06 05 04 03

Table of Contents

Lessons

What Happens When You Read

Reading is a process. It occurs over time—in the course of a few minutes, a few hours, a few days, or even longer if the book is very long or very good. Good readers know how to get "lost" in a book.

Visualizing Reading

Part of learning to be a better reader is seeing reading for what it really is. How do you picture yourself reading?

Directions: Draw a picture of yourself reading a really great book. Use "balloons" to show what you are thinking.

This is me reading.

Questions for Readers

Each time you pick up a book, you automatically ask yourself a series of questions. You do this without even realizing it. "Listening" to the questions you ask yourself can help you become a better reader.

Directions: Pick out a book from the classroom library that you'd like to read this year. Write the title and author's name on the lines below. Then ask yourself these questions about it.

Title:	**Author's Name:**
What are you reading about?	
Why are you reading?	
What do you want to get out of your reading?	
What kind of reading is it?	
Should you read slowly or quickly?	
What can you do if you don't understand something?	
How can you remember what you've read?	
How do you know if you've understood it?	
Should you read it more than once?	

The Reading Process

The reading process is the steps you follow to get more from a text.

Your Reading Process

Everyone has special habits when it comes to reading. What are yours? What do you do before, during, and after reading?

Directions: Describe your own reading process. Make notes or write in full sentences.

Before Reading

....

....

....

During Reading

....

....

....

After Reading

....

....

....

The Handbook's Reading Process

The *Reader's Handbook* contains many suggestions about a reading process. Some will be familiar to you, and some will be brand new. Think of the handbook's reading process as a road map you can refer to when reading. You'll use the "map" to prevent yourself from getting lost.

Directions: Skim pages 32–37 in the *Reader's Handbook*. Then use your own words to describe the reading process explained on these pages.

Before Reading

....

....

....

....

During Reading

....

....

....

....

After Reading

....

....

....

....

> If you get stuck, look at "Summing Up" on page 37 in your handbook.

Reading Know-how

The judgments, conclusions, and inferences you make every day are the same thinking skills you need to use when reading. These thinking skills are an important part of your reading know-how.

Thinking Skill 1: Making Inferences

Good readers make inferences, or reasonable guesses, about what is going on in a text.

Directions: Read the paragraph in the box. Then make inferences. Circle the answer that completes each sentence and write how you know the answer.

> **Sample Paragraph**
>
> Thirty young people gather in the school gym. They laugh and scream as they hang streamers and set tables along the wall. One group makes a stage from old wooden boards. Another group pesters the music teacher until he agrees to lend them microphones and amplifiers. Several young people set up a table near the door and cover it with a bright cloth. They put a ticket box on the table and hang signs that say "Restrooms this way" and "Refreshments this way."

My Inferences

The young people are preparing for: a dance   a gym meet   a test

How I know this:

The mood of the group is: angry   depressed   happy

How I know this:

The stage is for: the principal   a band   a visiting author

How I know this:

Thinking Skill 2: Drawing Conclusions

Drawing conclusions means taking bits of information and figuring out what they mean. It is sort of like looking at the clues on a treasure map to discover where the treasure might be.

Directions: Think again about the thirty young people at the school gym. Read the facts on the left. Write your conclusions on the right.

Drawing Conclusions

Facts		What I Concluded
Fact 1.	Thirty kids hang streamers in a school gym.	....
Fact 2.	One group makes a stage.	....
Fact 3.	The music teacher agrees to lend some microphones and amplifiers.	....
Fact 4.	Another group sets a table with a box for tickets.	....
Fact 5.	There is screaming and laughing.	....

Thinking Skill 3: Comparing and Contrasting

Comparing and contrasting means noticing how things are alike and different.

Directions: Put two different but similar objects on your desk, such as pieces of fruit or textbooks. Compare them in terms of size, shape, and appearance. Write your notes comparing them on this Venn Diagram.

Venn Diagram

Item A   Item B

Write notes that describe Item A here.   Write notes that describe Item B here.

Write what the two items have in common here.

Thinking Skill 4: Evaluating

When you evaluate, you make judgments. You say what you do and do not like about something. Then you explain your opinion.

Directions: Think about two classes you take in school. Tell which you think is more interesting. Explain why.

I think _____ is more interesting because _____

_____ .

_____

NAME ....

FOR USE WITH PAGES 43–46

Reading Actively

Being a good reader means staying on top of what you're reading. Active readers notice everything. They ask questions, make predictions, and connect the text to their own lives.

Ways of Reading Actively

Good readers mark, highlight, and make notes as they read. They react to the author's words and visualize the people, places, and things they're reading about.

As you read, ask yourself questions, make predictions, and relate to the selection. Try to make judgments and comparisons. Think about the conclusions you can draw from what you are reading.

You can read actively without writing anything down, but it's easier to keep track of what you're reading if you mark the text or take notes.

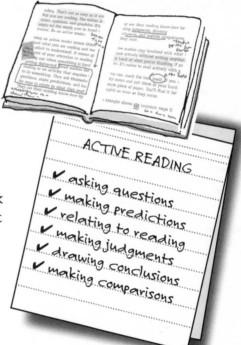

ACTIVE READING

✔ asking questions
✔ making predictions
✔ relating to reading
✔ making judgments
✔ drawing conclusions
✔ making comparisons

Directions: Turn to page 45 of the *Reader's Handbook*. Read the section called "Ways of Reading Actively." Then, read actively this short passage from "In Search of Epifano."

from "In Search of Epifano" by Rudolfo Anaya

The immense solitude of the desert swallowed her. She was only a moving shadow in the burning day. Overhead, vultures circled in the sky, the heat grew intense. She was alone on a dirt road she barely remembered. . . taking her bearings only by instinct, roughly following the north rim of the Cañon de Cobre, drawn by the thin line of the horizon, where the dull peaks of las montañas met the dull blue of the sky. Whirlwinds danced in her eyes, memories flooded at her soul.

1. Mark Highlight information about time and place.

2. Question Ask a question about the woman.

3. React Explain how this writing makes you feel.

4. Predict Predict what you think the woman is doing in the desert.

5. Visualize Make a sketch of the scene.

6. Clarify Write your inferences about the woman.

4. My prediction:

5. My sketch

2. My question:

3. How the writing makes me feel:

6. My inferences:

Reading Paragraphs

To analyze a paragraph, first find the subject, and then decide what the writer is saying about the subject. Follow these four steps.

Step 1: Read the paragraph.

Your first step is to do an active reading of the paragraph.

Directions: Read this paragraph from a short story by Judith Ortiz Cofer.

from "The Myth of the Latin Woman: I Just Met a Girl Named María" by Judith Ortiz Cofer

On a bus trip to London from Oxford University, where I was earning some graduate credits one summer, a young man, obviously fresh from a pub, spotted me and as if struck by inspiration went down on his knees in the aisle. With both hands over his heart he broke into an Irish tenor's rendition of "María" from *West Side Story*. My politely amused fellow passengers gave his lovely voice the round of gentle applause it deserved. Though I was not quite as amused, I managed my version of an English smile: no show of teeth, no extreme contortions of the facial muscles—I was at this time of my life practicing reserve and cool. Oh, that British control, how I coveted it. But María had followed me to London, reminding me of a prime fact of my life: you can leave the Island, master the English language, and travel as far as you can, but if you are a Latina, especially one like me who so obviously belongs to Rita Moreno's gene pool, the Island travels with you.

Highlight/Mark

What repeated words did you find?

Question

Ask yourself a question about the main idea of this paragraph.

Clarify

How does the author feel about the man who sings to her?

Step 2: Find the subject.

To find the subject, ask yourself: "What is this paragraph mostly about?"
You can find the subject by looking at these things:

- **the title**
- **the first sentence**
- **key or repeated words or names**

Directions: Answer these questions about the paragraph by Cofer. They can help you find the subject.

1. What does the title mean to you?

2. What is the first sentence about?

3. Who is telling the story?

4. What repeated words did you notice?

5. Who or what is the paragraph mostly about?

Step 3: Find the main idea.

Stated Main Idea

Some writers state the main idea directly. If this is the case, the paragraph has what is called a "stated main idea." Very often the stated main idea will be the first sentence or last sentence of the paragraph.

Directions: Reread the paragraph on page 15 from Cofer's story. Circle the main idea sentence. Then write it here.

Cofer's stated main idea is ....

....

....

....

I know this because ....

....

....

....

Implied Main Idea

Sometimes the main idea of a paragraph is implied. This means it's not directly stated. When this is the case, you need to make inferences, or reasonable guesses, about the main idea. Do this by asking yourself, "What is the writer trying to tell me about the subject?"

What is Cofer trying to tell you about her heritage? ....

....

....

....

....

Step 4: Find support.

Good writers support their main ideas with convincing facts and details. A Main Idea Organizer like the one below can help you see how a main idea and details work together.

Directions: Complete this organizer. Use the notes you made while reading Cofer's paragraph from "The Myth of the Latin Woman: I Just Met a Girl Named María."

Main Idea Organizer

Write Cofer's main idea here.

Main Idea

Detail	Detail	Detail

Write her supporting details here.

Reading History

When you read history, you read about people's hopes and fears and about conflict, leadership, and decision making.

Before Reading

To get the most out of a history text, you need a plan that can help you understand new facts, connect to what's being described, and keep track of what you're learning. Use the reading process and the strategy of note-taking to help you read and understand a textbook chapter called "A Declaration of Independence."

 Set a Purpose

When reading history, your purpose is to find answers to these five questions: *who, what, where, when,* and *why.*

• **Use the 5 W's as your purpose for reading.**

Directions: Ask five questions about "A Declaration of Independence." One question is done for you. You will answer your questions later.

◀ 5 W's Organizer ▶

WHO?	WHAT?	WHERE?	WHEN?	WHY?
		Where was the Declaration written?		

To set your purpose, write your questions here.

Textbooks

B Preview

During your preview, pay attention to the study guide, the first and last paragraphs, and terms set in bold type or repeated.

Directions: Preview by running your eyes over the document. Highlight names, dates, and repeated words.

Chapter 9 A Declaration of Independence

Study Guide

Main Idea: The Continental Congress needed a document declaring independence for the thirteen colonies.

Goals: As you read, look for answers to these questions:
1. Who wrote the Declaration?
2. What made this document necessary?
3. When was it signed, and by whom?

Words to Know
delegates
proposal
drafting
unalienable
parchment

The Second Continental Congress met in Philadelphia in May of 1775, a month after the American Revolution had begun (see Figure 9.1). At this meeting, **delegates,** or representatives, from the thirteen colonies agreed that they would have to act together if they were to defeat the British. After some discussion, the Congress agreed to create an American Continental Army. John Adams, the leader of the Massachusetts delegates, suggested that George Washington of Virginia become commander in chief. The other delegates agreed, and Washington was elected leader of the newly formed army.

Figure 9.1 Key Dates of the American Revolution

1765 British Parliament passes Stamp Act ·······························▸

1768 King George III sends soldiers to Boston, Massachusetts

1770 Boston Massacre

1773 Boston Tea Party

1774 First Continental Congress

1775 Second Continental Congress

1776 Declaration of Independence is completed

1778 France joins America in the fight against the British

1783 Treaty of Paris is signed, bringing an end to the American Revolution

Reading History ■

NAME ....

FOR USE WITH PAGES 66–83

A Committee Is Formed

In this same session of Congress, the delegates discussed ways to tell the British why they were seeking independence. One delegate made a **proposal,** or suggestion, that a formal document be drawn up by the Congress and delivered to the British. This document, he said, would set forth the reasons the colonists wanted to be free of British rule.

The other delegates agreed with this proposal. On June 11, 1776, a **drafting,** or writing, committee of the Continental Congress was formed to declare colonial independence from British rule. The committee included Thomas Jefferson, Benjamin Franklin, John Adams, Roger Sherman, and Robert Livingston.

Drafting the Declaration

The actual drafting of the document fell to Thomas Jefferson, who was known as a skilled writer. Although Jefferson was flattered by the committee's trust in him, he was nevertheless hesitant to take on the task of writing such an important document. After speaking with members of the committee, however, Jefferson knew he must accept the assignment.

Jefferson spent three weeks drafting the Declaration of Independence. In some places he struggled over wording, but for the most part he wrote with great confidence. His lines that "all men are created equal" and that they are all deserving of **unalienable,** or unchanging, rights including "life, liberty, and the pursuit of happiness" are now among the most famous words ever written.

The Signing of the Declaration of Independence, July 4, 1776

Stop and Record

Who *drafted the Declaration?* When *and* where *was it written? Make notes on your 5W's Organizer (page 23).*

First Responses to the Declaration

On July 1, 1776, Jefferson presented his Declaration to the drafting committee. Members suggested a few minor word changes. In particular, they wanted Jefferson to expand the list of charges against King George III.

Next, Jefferson showed the Declaration to the entire Continental Congress. They too asked Jefferson to make some minor changes, but for the most part, Jefferson's first draft became the final draft.

Jefferson's Declaration, which was titled "The Unanimous Declaration of the Thirteen United States of America," was printed onto **parchment** (paper made from the skin of a sheep or goat) by Thomas Matlock of Philadelphia. This important document was formally signed by members of the Continental Congress three days later, on July 4, a date which is remembered today as Independence Day.

Stop and Record

What *was the purpose of the Declaration of Independence?*
Why *is July 4 celebrated as Independence Day? Make notes on your 5 W's Organizer (page 23).*

C Plan

You probably found some quick answers to your 5 W's on your preview. As you do your careful reading, watch for additional information that relates to these questions.

• **Use a 5 W's Organizer to keep track of what you learn.**

During Reading

Now go back and do a careful reading of "A Declaration of Independence." Take notes as you go.

D Read with a Purpose

Be sure to keep in mind your reading purpose. You are looking for answers to *who, what, where, when,* and *why.*

Directions: As you read, think about your purpose questions. Answer your questions on this organizer.

5 W's Organizer

Who	What	Where	When	Why

Using the Strategy

A 5 W's Organizer is one way of organizing your notes during reading. But there are many note-taking options.

- **Paragraph-by-paragraph notes can help you organize facts from each paragraph of an article.**

Directions: Find at least one important fact from each paragraph of "A Declaration of Independence." Record what you find on this chart.

Paragraph-by-Paragraph Notes Chart

Paragraph	Facts I found
1	Delegates from the thirteen states agreed that they would have to act together if they were to defeat the British.
2	
3	
4	
5	
6	
7	
8	

Understanding How
History Textbooks Are Organized

Many history chapters and articles open with a study guide or goals box. These can help you think about what you've learned.

Directions: Review the 5 W's Organizer on page 23. Then answer the questions.

1. Who wrote the Declaration?

2. What made this document necessary?

3. When was it signed, and by whom?

E Connect

Find a way to connect with the reading.

- **Imagining yourself a part of history can help you make a strong connection to the text.**

Directions: Put yourself in Thomas Jefferson's shoes. Ask yourself the questions that follow.

1. What was the hardest part about writing the Declaration?

2. What was the easiest?

Textbooks

After Reading

After you finish reading, take a moment to decide whether you've understood the text.

F **Pause and Reflect**

Return to your 5 W's Organizer. Are there parts of the chapter that you had trouble with?

• **Ask yourself, "How well did I meet my purpose?"**

<u>**Directions:**</u> Answer these two questions about the chapter "A Declaration of Independence."

1. Which parts of the chapter did you find easiest to understand?

2. Which parts were most challenging? Why?

NAME

 **G Reread**

Use the rereading to help you keep track of important facts and details.

• At the rereading stage, create an Outline of the chapter or article.

Directions: Complete this Outline. Refer to your notes and the reading.

Outline

I. A Committee Is Formed

Detail 1: ....

Detail 2: ....

II. Drafting the Declaration

Detail 1: ....

Detail 2: ....

III. First Responses to the Declaration

Detail 1: ....

Detail 2: ....

H Remember

It's important that you remember what you read in your history text.

• To remember a history text, share what you've learned.

Directions: Write three facts from the chapter to share with a friend.

1. ....

2. ....

3. ....

Reading Geography

If you're having trouble with geography, it might be because of how you're reading the textbook. Practice reading and responding to a geography chapter here.

Before Reading

On these pages, you'll use the reading process and the strategy of using graphic organizers to help you read and respond to a geography chapter about the physical geography of Southeast Asia. Take what you learn here and apply it to your own reading.

 A **Set a Purpose**

Your purpose for reading a geography chapter is twofold: Find out the subject of the chapter, and learn why the information is important.

• **To set your purpose, turn the title of the geography chapter into a question.**

Write your purpose for reading these pages from a chapter called "The Physical Geography of Southeast Asia"

My purpose: ....

....

....

 B **Preview**

A preview can show you what to expect during your careful reading.

Directions: Preview the following two pages from the geography chapter. Make notes on page 30 about the subject, key terms, first paragraph, and the graphics.

11 The Physical Geography of Southeast Asia

Preview

Key Terms

cataclysmic
cordillera
flora
fauna
archipelago

Places to Locate

Indochinese Peninsula
the Philippines
Malay Peninsula
Singapore
Bay of Bengal

Read and Learn—

1. the natural forces that shaped Southeast Asia.

2. geographical similarities and differences between mainland and island Southeast Asia.

3. the natural resources and climate of Southeast Asia.

Southeast Asia is a region of Asia that includes the Indochinese and Malay peninsulas and several nearby island groups. The region is bordered on the north by China; on the south by the Indian Ocean; on the east by the South Pacific Ocean; and on the west by the Indian Ocean, the Bay of Bengal, and the Indian subcontinent. Southeast Asia includes the countries of Brunei, Cambodia (Kâmpuchéa), Indonesia, Laos, Malaysia, Myanmar (formerly known as Burma), the Philippines, Singapore, Thailand, and Vietnam **(see Figure 11.1)**.

SOUTHEAST ASIA: COUNTRY PROFILE		
Country	**Population**	**Landmass**
Brunei	300,000	2,035 sq. mi.
Cambodia	10,800,000	68,154 sq. mi.
Indonesia	207,400,000	705,190 sq. mi.
Laos	5,300,000	89,110 sq. mi.
Malaysia	22,200,000	126,860 sq. mi.
Myanmar	47,100,000	253,880 sq. mi.
Philippines	75,300,000	115,120 sq. mi.
Singapore	5,900,000	236 sq. mi.
Thailand	61,000,000	197,250 sq. mi.
Vietnam	77,500,000	125,670 sq. mi.

Figure 11. 1

The Land

Southeast Asia was formed by the collision of the Eurasian, Philippine, and IndoAustralian tectonic plates. The collision took place millions of years ago and occurred over time, rather than as one **cataclysmic**, or sudden, event.

The clashing of the plates where India joined Asia forced up the Himalaya Mountains. This in turn created river valleys and **cordilleras,** or parallel mountain ranges, in the Indochinese Peninsula.

Southeast Asia can be divided into mainland and island countries. These countries are quite distinct from one another. Each has its own language, of course, and its own distinctive **flora,** or plants, and **fauna,** or animals.

Mainland and Island Southeast Asia

The countries of Vietnam, Laos, Cambodia, and Myanmar lie entirely on the Indochinese Peninsula. Thailand lies mainly on the Indochinese Peninsula, but also trails southward to the Malay Peninsula **(see Figure 11.2)**.

The islands of Southeast Asia are numerous and varied. Singapore is an island located off the southern tip of the Malay Peninsula. A separate island country, Indonesia, is composed of 13,677 small islands that stretch from the Indian Ocean to Papua New Guinea. The Philippines, which is an **archipelago** (a group of islands), is composed of 7,107 islands. Brunei, on the north edge of the island of Borneo, is also an island country of Southeast Asia.

Map Search   **Figure 11.2 Southeast Asia**

1. What region includes Vietnam, Cambodia, Laos, and Myanmar?
2. What is the capital of Myanmar?
3. Where is Manila located?

The subject of the chapter:
....

Key terms:
....

The first paragraph tells me this:
....

I noticed this about the graphics:
....

C   Plan

Your next step is to choose a strategy and make a reading plan.

- **Use graphic organizers to keep track of important information in a chapter.**

Directions: Complete this K-W-L Chart. Write what you already know about the geography of Southeast Asia in Column 1. Write what you want to know in Column 2. Save Column 3 for later.

K-W-L Chart

What I **K**now	What I **W**ant to Know	What I **L**earned

During Reading

Now go back and do a careful reading of the geography pages. As you read, write important facts and details in Column 3 of your K-W-L Chart.

D   Read with a Purpose

Remember to keep your purpose in mind as you read. Your goal is to find out what the chapter is about and why this information is important.

Using the Strategy

Many kinds of graphic organizers work well with geography textbooks. Choose the organizer that works best for you.

• A Concept Map can help you explore important ideas in the reading.

<u>**Directions:**</u> Explore important ideas and details about Southeast Asia on this Concept Map.

Concept Map

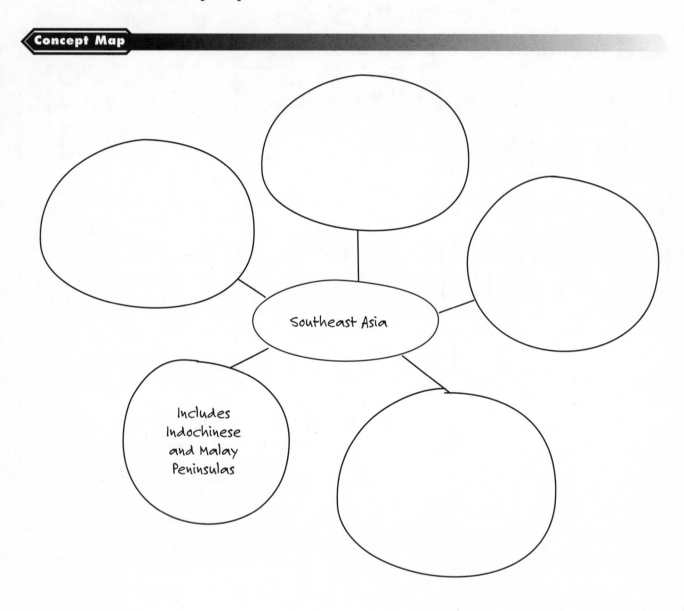

Southeast Asia

Includes Indochinese and Malay Peninsulas

Understanding How
Geography Textbooks Are Organized

Geography textbooks are usually organized around topics and graphics.

1. Topic Organization In most geography chapters, you will find several key topics. Within each topic there may be two or more subpoints.

<u>Directions:</u> Look at the sample Outline on page 94 of your handbook. Then complete this Outline using notes from the reading.

Textbooks

◄ Outline

I. The Land

    A. Formed by collision of tectonic plates

    B.

    C.

II. Mainland and Island Southeast Asia

    A.

    B.

    C.

2. Use of Graphics In addition to paying attention to key topics, you must also look carefully at the maps, graphs, tables, photographs, and other visual helps that are scattered throughout a chapter.

<u>Directions:</u> Look at the chart on page 29. Write one sentence that summarizes the point of the visual. Then do the same for the map on page 30.

One-sentence Summary

Chart:

Map:

 **Connect**

Making personal connections to a geography text can help you understand and stay interested in what you're reading.

• **As you read, make notes about information that you find interesting, surprising, or puzzling.**

Directions: Record your connections to the Southeast Asia reading here.

I was interested in these parts of the reading:

....

....

....

I found this information surprising:

....

....

....

I'm puzzled by this:

....

....

After Reading

After you finish reading, stop and consider what you've learned.

 Pause and Reflect

Begin by reflecting on your reading purpose.

• **After you finish a geography chapter, ask yourself, "How well did I meet my purpose?"**

Directions: Return to Column 3 of your K-W-L Chart (page 31). Note what you learned. Then decide whether or not you've met your reading purpose. Circle *have* or *have not* and explain.

I *have / have not* met my reading purpose. Here's why:

....

....

34

NAME

G Reread

Even the best readers can take in and retain only so much on a first reading. For this reason, it's a good idea to look back and reread.

• A powerful rereading strategy to use with geography is note-taking.

Directions: Reread the textbook pages. Write one question about Southeast Asia on the front of each Study Card. Then exchange books with a classmate. Have him or her answer the questions you've written.

◄ Study Cards

Textbooks

Remember

After you finish a reading, figure out a way to remember what you've learned.

• **Creating a practice test can help you remember important information.**

Directions: Create a practice test that covers the material in the Southeast Asia reading. Then turn the book upside down and make an answer key. One question has been done for you.

Practice Test for "The Physical Geography of Southeast Asia"

1. What is a cordillera?

a. a small Mexican town   b. where two rivers meet

c. a type of rock   d. a chain of mountains

2.

a.   b.

c.   d.

3.

a.   b.

c.   d.

4.

a.   b.

c.   d.

5.

a.   b.

c.   d.

Answer Key   1.   2.   3.   4.   5.

Reading  Science

If you're having trouble understanding science, it might be because of how you're reading the textbook. Good students know how to get more information from every page. Practice the strategies they use here.

Textbooks

Before Reading

Use the reading process and the strategy of note-taking to help you read and understand a science textbook chapter on insects.

 A

Set a Purpose

When you read a science chapter, your purpose is to find the subject and what the author has to say about it.

- **To set your purpose, ask a question about the subject, or what the reading is about.**

Directions: Write your purpose for reading "Insects of the World" here. Then make a prediction about the chapter. What do you expect to learn?

My purpose: ....

....

....

....

I think the reading will be about: ....

....

....

Here's why: ....

....

....

B Preview

The title of a science chapter is your first clue about its subject. The text features on this checklist will give you additional clues.

Directions: Place a check beside each text feature after you look at it. Then make some notes about your preview on the chart below.

- ☐ headings

- ☐ boxed items

- ☐ words in boldface or repeated words

- ☐ any photos, maps, diagrams, and so on

- ☐ first and last paragraphs

Preview Chart

The titles and headings tell me . . .	I noticed these repeated words . . .

"Insects of the World"

The boxed items and diagram tell me . . .	The first and last paragraphs tell me . . .

SECTION 3 Insects of the World

RESEARCH

• Check your library or do an Internet search for facts about the Africanized honeybee. Write what you find in your science journal.

DISCOVER

• Learn about the appearance and characteristics of insects.
• Understand how insects can help and hurt humans.
• Focus on the Africanized honeybee.

GOALS

1. Learn the physical characteristics of insects.
2. Learn the habits and habitats of Africanized honeybees.

Key Terms
entomologists
class
phylum
invertebrates
exoskeletons
colonies
swarms

Tip for Reading *As you read, make a list of insect characteristics.*

Understanding Insects

The world is full of insects. You know that, of course. But did you know that there are actually billions of "bugs" out there? Did you know that some insects are as big as rats and some are too tiny to be seen by the human eye? And did you know that insects' lives are every bit as complicated, surprising, and exciting as the lives we humans live?

Scientists know a lot about insects. Much of our information comes from **entomologists,** the scientists who study insects. By definition, an insect is any member of the **class Insecta. Insecta** is the largest class of the **phylum Arthropoda (see Figure 3.1).**

CLASS OR GROUP = INSECTS
Insects are part of the phylum Arthropoda. Arthropods are animals without a backbone. Spiders, shrimp, and lobsters are also arthropods.

Figure 3.1

Characteristics

Insects are **invertebrates.** This means that they are animals without backbones. All insects have segmented bodies and jointed legs. Some insects, such as beetles, have what are called **exoskeletons.** An exoskeleton is a hard outer skin that protects the soft inner body of the invertebrate in much the same way that a knight's armor protects the knight.

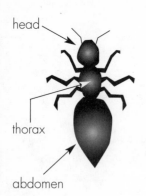

head

thorax

abdomen

**Figure 3.2
The three major
parts of an
insect's body.**

The main difference between insects and other arthropods is that the body of an insect is divided into three major parts **(see Figure 3.2).** An insect's head contains the mouthparts, eyes, and antennae. The thorax usually contains three pairs of legs and often one or two pairs of wings. The many-segmented abdomen contains the digestive and reproductive organs.

Appearance and Habits

Most insects are quite small. Although the average size is 0.2 inches (6 millimeters) in length, some insects can be quite large. The feather-winged beetles and parasitic wasps, for example, can grow to the size of a small bird.

You might be surprised to learn that most insects ignore humans. They have their own lives to lead, in their own **colonies,** or societies. Some live underground, and some build nests high in the rooftops. Some fly only at night, and some fly only in the early hours of the morning. Some insects, such as the mayfly, can live up to 50 years. Others, such as the domestic housefly, have a life span of approximately one month.

Insects and Humans Together

When people think of insects, they tend to think of the familiar pests or disease carriers such as houseflies and mosquitoes, but many insects are actually quite helpful to humans. Among other things, insects pollinate plants and produce useful substances such as honey. Insects control pests, act as scavengers, and serve as food for other animals.

Perhaps most important, insects help us learn about ourselves and our world. Much of our knowledge about genetics and population comes from studies entomologists did with fruit flies and flour beetles. Scientists also use insects to learn about natural processes such as digestion.

Of course, some insects can cause trouble for humans. Mosquitoes and other flying insects can spread disease. Stinging insects, such as wasps and hornets, will use their stingers if they feel their hive is threatened. A particular type of bee, called the Africanized honeybee, may even kill a large animal or human if provoked.

Focus on "Killer Bees"

Every spring and summer you can find newspaper and magazine articles about swarms of "killer" bees that are on their way to the United States. Do these insects really exist? And if so, why do they want to kill humans?

"Killer" bees are actually Africanized honeybees, a close relation to the gently buzzing honeybees that live in the United States. But Africanized honeybees are not really "killers." Although they do travel in **swarms,** or groups, most Africanized honeybees keep to themselves.

Appearance and Habits

Africanized honeybees look very much like other honeybees, although they are a bit smaller in size **(see Figure 3.3).** Like other bees, they become angry only when they think their hive is threatened. But Africanized honeybees can sense a threat sooner and become angry more quickly. When they attack, they move in swarms. Entire swarms have been known to attack animals and humans.

The Origin of Africanized Honeybees

Where do Africanized honeybees come from? Believe it or not, they come from scientists who were simply trying to do their jobs.

In 1956 a group of scientists cut down a hive in an African jungle and brought it to Brazil. They wanted to see if they could mate the African queens with the Brazilian bees. They were hoping to create a new kind of bee that would be a better honey producer.

During the experiment, however, some African queen bees were accidentally released into the wild. In the

Figure 3.3 An Africanized honeybee.

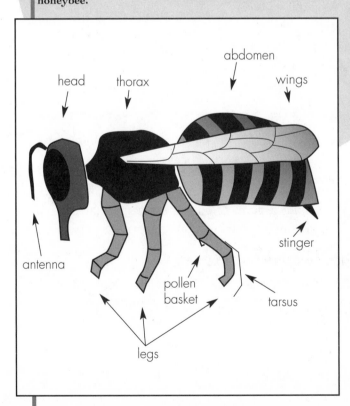

head   thorax   abdomen   wings

antenna

pollen basket

stinger

tarsus

legs

weeks and months that followed, the African queens mated with the Brazilian bees. Their offspring became known as "Africanized" honeybees.

These new bees were quick to anger. They also stayed angry longer than the Brazilian bees and had a tendency to swarm. When several people were attacked by swarms, the Brazilians began calling the Africanized bees "killer" bees.

Scientists tracking the Africanized bees learned that these bees did not want to share their territory with other honeybees. The gentler honeybees, known as European honeybees, were forced out of Brazil by the Africanized bees. In just a few years, more than a billion Africanized bees were alive and well in South and Central America, and their European counterparts were nowhere to be found.

Africanized Honeybees in the United States

Although most people don't realize it, Africanized honeybees have been in the United States for years. So far, their colonies have been small and easily contained. Still, U.S. beekeepers are worried. They know that the Africanized honey bees pose a threat to their honey business. They are afraid that the Africanized bees will drive the European bees out of their hives, just as they did in South and Central America. The result will be hives filled with bees that will fight to the death to protect their honey.

 Plan

After previewing the chapter, make a plan. Choose a strategy that can help you read, understand, and remember what you've learned.

> • **Use the strategy of note-taking to get *more* from a science text.**

Look at the sample Thinking Tree on page 107 of your handbook. Use the Thinking Tree on the next page to organize information as you read.

During Reading

Now do a careful reading of "Insects of the World." Write your notes on the Thinking Tree. Use the chapter headings from the book as your guide to what's important.

D Read with a Purpose

Keep in mind that your purpose is to discover the subject and what is said about the subject.

Directions: Use the organizer below for your notes about the chapter.

Thinking Tree

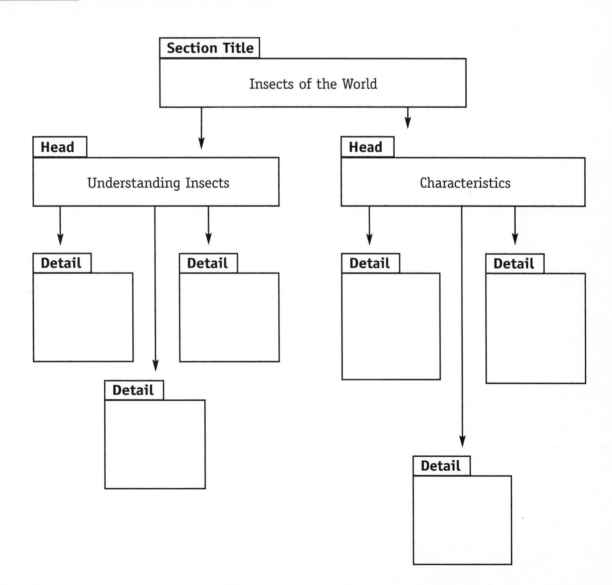

Section Title

Insects of the World

Head

Understanding Insects

Head

Characteristics

Detail

Detail

Detail

Detail

Detail

Detail

Using the Strategy

There are all different ways to take notes. Choose the method that's best for you.

• **Key Word Notes help you study and organize information around key concepts.**

Directions: Complete this organizer. Refer to your notes from the reading.

Key Word Notes

Key Words/Concepts	Text Notes
Insect habits	
Insects and humans	
Colonies	
Africanized honeybees	
"Killer" bees	
swarm	

Understanding How Science Texts Are Organized

Textbook writers often use cause-effect order to explain important science concepts. Watch for cause-effect relationships as you read.

Directions: Use this diagram to show what happened when the African queen bees were mistakenly released in Brazil.

Cause-Effect Organizer

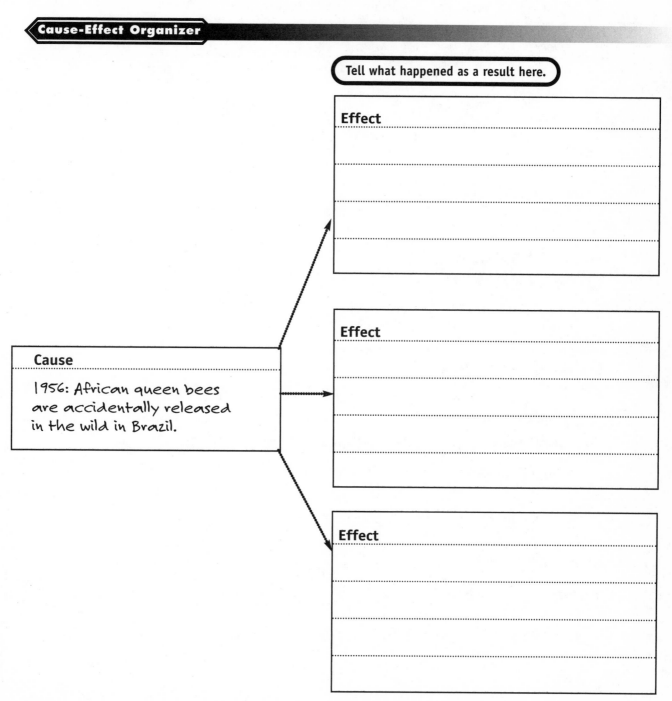

Tell what happened as a result here.

Effect

Effect

Cause

1956: African queen bees are accidentally released in the wild in Brazil.

Effect

E Connect

Good readers think about how the information in a science chapter relates to them personally.

• **As you read, make notes about things that are familiar or of interest to you.**

Directions: Write your reactions to the chapter on insects. What surprised you? What would you like to learn more about?

My reactions: ....

....

....

....

....

After Reading

When you finish reading a science chapter, take the time to be sure you've learned everything you needed to learn.

F Pause and Reflect

Return to your reading purpose and ask yourself what you've learned about the subject.

• **After you finish reading, ask yourself, "Did I meet my purpose?"**

Directions: Answer *yes* or *no* to these questions.

1. Do I know the main topic of the chapter? ....

2. Do I understand what point the writer is making about this topic? ....

3. Can I explain the key terms? ....

4. Do the graphics, pictures, and captions make sense? ....

 **Reread**

If you can't answer *yes* to each question, you need to return to the chapter and do some rereading.

• Use the rereading strategy of skimming to help you find answers to specific questions.

Directions: Skim the reading for details that support the main idea that insects can help us.

Textbooks

Main Idea Organizer

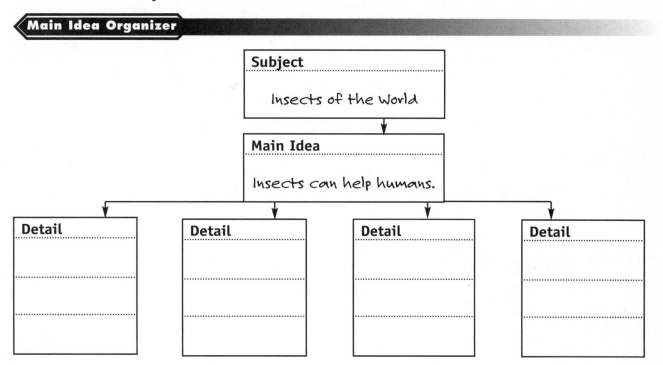

H Remember

Science is a "hands-on" subject. You can take what you learn and create something interesting.

• To remember a science chapter, make a sketch.

Directions: Sketch an insect here. Write three characteristics under your sketch.

Three characteristics: ....

Reading  Math

To be a good math student, you need to be a good reader. You need to be the kind of reader who knows how to get more out of a text.

Before Reading

Begin by establishing your purpose for reading. Use the reading process and the strategy of visualizing and thinking aloud to read a math feature. A question about the subject will make a good purpose question.

 Set a Purpose

- **To set your purpose, turn the title of the chapter or page into a question.**

Directions: Write your purpose for reading a math feature called "Order of Operations." Then tell what you already know about the subject.

My purpose: ....

....

....

What I already know about the subject: ....

....

....

B Preview

It's very important that you preview a math text before you begin reading. Your preview can remind you of what you already know and help you decide what you need to learn.

• Use a K-W-L Chart for your preview notes.

<u>Directions:</u> Preview the two math pages that follow. Pay attention to headings, boxed items, models, diagrams, and examples. Make some notes on this K-W-L Chart.

K-W-L Chart

What I **K**now	What I **W**ant to Know	What I **L**earned

Write what you already know here.

Write what you need to find out about the subject here.

Make notes in this section after your careful reading.

Math Feature

1.7

Order of Operations

Study Guide

Goal
Learn how to evaluate a variable expression.

Learn how to use order of operations.

Key Terms
expression
numerical
  expression
variable
  expression
evaluating the
  expression

Evaluating Variable Expressions

An **expression** is a collection of numbers, variables, and symbols such as +, –, x, and ÷. An expression that has only numbers and symbols is a **numerical expression.** For example:

$$(3 \times 3) + 4 = 13$$

An expression that has one or more variables is a **variable expression.** For example:

$$16 - (2 \times n)$$

Finding the value of an expression is called **evaluating the expression.**

Example: **Evaluating a Variable Expression**

Evaluate 10 + (2 x n) for the given values of n.

a. $n = 1$ **b.** $n = 3$

Solution

Value of n	Substitute	Numerical Expression
a. $n = 1$	$10 + (2 \times 1) =$	$10 + 2 = 12$
b. $n = 3$	$10 + (2 \times 3) =$	$10 + 6 = 16$

Double-check √√ **Evaluating Variable Expressions**

This is how you

evaluate a

variable expression:

Evaluating an

expression is

Use your calculator to evaluate each expression.

1. $(2 \times 6) - 10 =$

2. $(5 \times 1) + (5 \times 4) =$

3. $40 - (3 \times 4) + 2 =$

4. $(2 \times 8) \div 2 =$

NAME

Math Feature
1.7

Using Order of Operations

The value of an expression with two or more operations depends on the order in which you do the operations. For this reason, there are rules for ordering operations to evaluate expressions.

Rules for Ordering Operations

1. First, do the operations with grouping symbols.
2. Next, multiply and divide from left to right.
3. Finally, add and subtract from left to right.

Example: Using Order of Operations

a. $24 - 6 \times 3 = 24 - 18 = 6$
First multiply: 6×3.
Then subtract: $24 - 18$.

b. $(4 + 8) \div 3 \times 2 = 12 \div 3 \times 2 = 4 \times 2 = 8$
First evaluate expression inside of parentheses: $(4 + 8)$
Then divide: $12 \div 3$.
Finish by multiplying: 4×2.

Double-check √√ **Using Order of Operations**

Here are the rules for order of operation:

Use your calculator to evaluate each expression.

1. Evaluate $15 - (m \times 2)$ for the given values of m.
  a. $m = 4$ **b.** $m = 6$ **c.** $m = 1$ **d.** $m = 7$

2. Evaluate the expressions.
  a. $9 - 3 \div 3 + 3 =$
  b. $2 \times (7 + 6) =$
  c. $24 \div 2 (1 + 4) =$
  d. $w = 17 + (30 - 14) =$

C Plan

In a math text, every word—no matter how small or simple—is important. This means you must read slowly and carefully and take notes. Choose a strategy that can help you find out what you need to know.

• **Use the strategy of visualizing and thinking aloud to help you solve math problems and memorize rules and formulas.**

During Reading

Visualizing means making a mental image of a problem. Thinking aloud means talking yourself through a problem. It can be as simple as saying, "First I do this, next I do that, and finally I arrive at the answer."

D Read with a Purpose

Now go back and do a careful reading of the two math pages. Keep your purpose in mind as you read. Make notes.

Using the Strategy

Directions: On the lines below, write a Think Aloud that explains how you would use order of operations to solve this problem:

$$10 + 7(6 - 2) =$$

Think Aloud

Understanding How
Math Texts Are Organized

Textbooks

Study Guide

Goal

Learn how to evaluate
a variable expression.

Learn how to use order
of operations.

Key Terms

expression
numerical expression
variable expression
evaluating the expression

Most math chapters and features open with a study guide
or goals box that lists key terms and objectives. The box
at the left is one example.

After you finish your careful reading, take a second look
at the box on the opening page. Check to see that you've
met each goal and learned each term.

__Directions:__ Answer these questions using notes from
your reading.

1. What is an expression?

....

....

....

....

2. What is the difference between a numerical expression and a variable expression?

....

....

....

....

3. In your own words, tell the order of operations used to evaluate an expression.

....

....

....

Connect

You can make a math problem more interesting and easier to remember if you relate it to your own life or an experience you've had.

• **Making a connection to the math problem will help you solve it.**

Directions: Read the problem and sample connection on page 128. Then create a connection for the problems below. Use an event or experience from your own life.

Problem	Connection
1. $3 \times (30 - 2) =$	
2. $3(6 + 9) =$	
3. $m = 100 \div (30 - 5)$	

After Reading

At this point, take a moment to reflect on what you've learned.

F Pause and Reflect

Return to your reading purpose. Ask yourself what you've learned about order of operations.

• **When you finish reading, ask yourself: "Did I meet my purpose?"**

<u>Directions:</u> Check *yes* or *no* in response to each question.

Purpose Checklist

Yes	No	
☐	☐	I understand the key terms.
☐	☐	I can explain what each term means.
☐	☐	I understand the sample problems.
☐	☐	I can take what I've learned and use it to solve the exercises.

G Reread

Unless you're a math whiz, you will need to spend some time thinking and rethinking the rules and strategies you've learned. Return to the parts of the text that you're not sure of and do some rereading.

• **A powerful rereading strategy to use is note-taking.**

<u>Directions:</u> Read the terms in the left column. Write definitions in the middle column and examples on the right. One has been done for you.

Key Word Notes

Key Terms	Definitions	Examples
expression	a collection of numbers, variables, and symbols	$36 \div n = 6$
numerical expression		
variable expression		
order of operations		

Remember

New math concepts you learn hinge on concepts that you studied previously. For this reason, find a way to remember what you've learned.

• **Creating sample tests can help you remember important information.**

Directions: Create a sample test that explores one of the concepts in this lesson. Give the test to a partner and see how well he or she does. Your partner should solve the problem and explain how to solve it.

Sample Test: _____   ← ⟨ **Write the strategy to be tested here.** ⟩ ....

1. $4 \times 5 + 10 = 30$

   First multiply 4 by 5. Then add 10.

2. ....

   ....

3. ....

   ....

4. ....

   ....

5. ....

   ....

6. ....

   ....

7. ....

   ....

8. ....

   ....

9. ....

   ....

10. ....

    ....

Focus on Science Concepts

In science and other subjects, concept *is a word for "big idea." Follow these steps to read and understand a science concept.*

Step 1: Learn key terms.

To understand a science concept, you must first understand the key terms.

Directions: Look at the nitrogen cycle diagram below. Write key terms in the word bank. Use a dictionary to define each term.

Word Bank

Word	Definition
Nitrogen	

Nitrogen Cycle

N_2
Nitrogen in the air
N_2

N_2 N_2 N_2 N_2 N_2 N_2

Plants use nitrates and other compounds.

Dead animals and plants decay.

Nitrogen returns to the atmosphere. This process is called *nitrification*.

Nitrates and other nitrogen compounds are formed.

Nitrogen is deposited into the soil and the roots of some plants.

NO_3 NO_3 NO_3

Step 2: Understand the steps in the process.

Your next step is to understand how the process works.

Directions: Write the steps of the nitrogen cycle here. Include key terms from your word bank in a Concept Map.

Concept Map

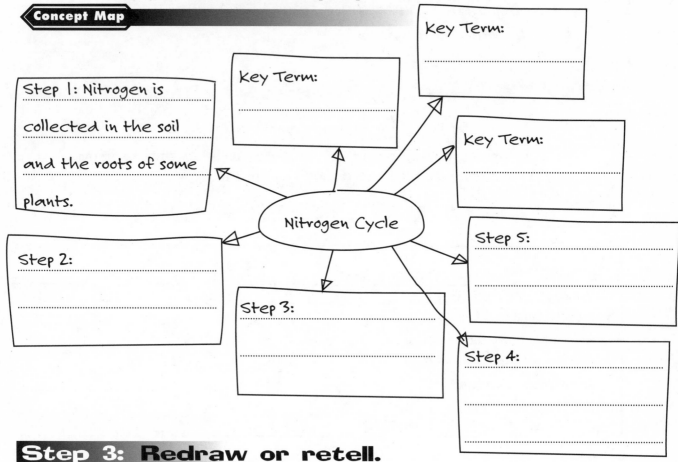

Step 1: Nitrogen is collected in the soil and the roots of some plants.

Key Term:

Key Term:

Key Term:

Nitrogen Cycle

Step 2:

Step 3:

Step 5:

Step 4:

Step 3: Redraw or retell.

Making the scientific concept "your own" can help you remember it. Try redrawing or retelling what it's about.

Directions: Look at the redrawing of cell division on page 142 of your handbook. Then use the same technique to redraw the nitrogen cycle.

Nitrogen Cycle

NAME

Focus on Word Problems

Most word problems are solved in basically the same way.
Use this four-step plan.

Step 1: Read.

Begin by reading the problem at least twice. Figure out what it is asking for.

Directions: Read this word problem. Take notes on the "topic," the "given," and the "unknown." Reread page 144 of your handbook if you need help.

◀ **Sample Word Problem**

1. Lisa is the chairperson for the Elmwood Middle School dance. Eighty percent of the seventh-graders have said they will come to the dance. If there are a total of 60 seventh-graders at Elmwood, how many will attend the dance?	**Topic** (What the problem is about): **Given** (What is known about the topic): **Unknown** (What you need to find out):

Step 2: Plan.

Next, choose a strategy that will help you solve the problem. The best all-purpose strategy to use with word problems is visualizing.

Directions: Make a sketch that shows the problem.

Step 3: Solve.

As a third step, use your notes and sketch to help you write a numerical expression.

Directions: Write a numerical expression for the Elmwood Middle School dance problem.

My numerical expression:

Step 4: Check.

Always check your work. The strategy of thinking aloud can help.

Directions: Write a Think Aloud that shows how you solved the problem.

Think Aloud

Let's see. I need to find out how many students are going to attend the dance,

so I

Reading an Essay

*Essays are everywhere, especially in your schoolbooks.
As a critical reader, your job is to understand the subject
and thesis, or main idea, of the essay. Then you need
to decide how you feel about the message of the essay.*

Before Reading

Practice reading, responding to, and evaluating an essay here. Use the reading process and strategy of outlining to help you get more from the essay "How Can America Be My Home?"

A Set a Purpose

To set your purpose, ask a question about the author's message and what you think about it.

• Ask a question about the title, author, or main idea of the essay.

Directions: Write your purpose for reading "How Can America Be My Home?" here.

My purpose: ....

....

....

B Preview

Always preview before you begin reading. Look for clues about the subject of the essay. Pay particular attention to the title, first paragraph, and any background information. Also watch for headings and repeated words or phrases.

Nonfiction

Directions: Preview "How Can America Be My Home?" Write your preview notes on this Web.

Web

Author's name:

Essay subject:

Background information:

"How Can America Be My Home?"

Details from the

first paragraph:

Details from the

last paragraph:

Repeated words:

C Plan

After your preview, make a plan for reading. What's the best way to understand the author's message and decide how you feel about it?

- **The strategy of outlining can help you keep track of details that relate to the author's message.**

During Reading

Most essays contain three parts: an introduction, a body, and a conclusion. Make notes of each part as you read. Then use your notes to help you create your outline.

D Read with a Purpose

Remember that you want to find out the author's thesis, or message. The thesis statement usually appears in the introduction or conclusion.

Directions: Now do a careful reading of Lee Chew's essay. Watch for his thesis in the concluding paragraph. Make notes on this Outline as you read.

Outline

I. Introduction

....A. Detail

....B. Detail

II. Body

....A. Support for thesis

....B. Support for thesis

....C. Support for thesis

III. Conclusion

....A. Thesis statement

....B. Concluding detail

"How Can America Be My Home?"

is an excerpt from an essay that was first published
in a magazine called *The Independent* in 1903.

*The author of the essay, Lee Chew, was born in the Chinese province
of Canton, on the banks of the Si-Kiang River. Chew traveled to America
when he was sixteen years old. He came in search of wealth and opportunity
and the dream of improving his life and the lives of his family back home.
In his essay, Chew explains that the America he saw in real life was nothing
like the America of his dreams.*

It was twenty years ago when I came to this country, and I worked for two years
as a servant, getting at the last $35 a month. I sent money home to comfort my parents,
but though I dressed well and lived well and had pleasure, going quite often to the
Chinese theater and to dinner parties in Chinatown, I saved $50 in the first six months,
$90 in the second, $120 in the third and $150 in the fourth. So I had $410 at the end
of two years, and I was now ready to start in business.

When I first opened a laundry it was in company with a partner, who had been
in the business for some years. We went to a town about 500 miles inland, where
a railroad was building. We got a board shanty and worked for the men employed by
the railroads. Our rent cost us $10 a month and food nearly $5 a week each, for all
food was dear and we wanted the best of everything—we lived principally on rice,
chickens, ducks and pork, and did our own cooking. The Chinese take naturally to
cooking. It cost us about $50 for our furniture and apparatus, and we made close upon
$60 a week, which we divided between us. We had to put up with many insults and
some frauds, as men would come in and claim parcels that did not belong to them,
saying they had lost their tickets, and would fight if they did not get what they asked
for. Sometimes we were taken before Magistrates and fined for losing shirts that we
had never seen. . . .

Stop and Record

Make some notes in the "Introduction" section of the Outline (page 63).

When the railroad construction gang moved on, we went with them. The men were
rough and prejudiced against us, but not more so than in the big Eastern cities. It is
only lately in New York that the Chinese have been able to discontinue putting wire

"How Can America Be My Home?" by Lee Chew, continued

screens in front of their windows, and at the present time the street boys are still breaking the windows of Chinese laundries all over the city, while the police seem to think it a joke.

We were three years with the railroad, and then went to the mines, where we made plenty of money in gold dust, but had a hard time, for many of the miners were wild men who carried revolvers and after drinking would come into our place to shoot and steal shirts, for which we had to pay. One of these men hit his head hard against a flat iron and all the miners came and broke up our laundry, chasing us out of town. They were going to hang us. We lost all our property and $365 in money, which members of the mob must have found.

Luckily most of our money was in the hands of Chinese bankers in San Francisco. I drew $500 and went East to Chicago, where I had a laundry for three years, during which I increased my capital to $2,500. . . .

The ordinary laundry shop is generally divided into three rooms. In front is the room where the customers are received, behind that a bedroom and in the back the work shop, which is also the dining room and kitchen. The stove and cooking utensils are the same as those of the Americans.

Work in a laundry begins early on Monday morning at about seven o'clock. There are generally two men, one of whom washes while the other does the ironing. The man who irons does not start in till Tuesday, as the clothes are not ready for him to begin till that time. So he has Sundays and Mondays as holidays. The man who does the washing finishes up on Friday night, and so he has Saturday and Sunday. Each works only five days a week, but those are long days—from seven o'clock in the morning till midnight. . . .

Recently there has been organized among us the Oriental Club, composed of our most intelligent and influential men. We hope for a great improvement in social conditions by its means, as it will discuss matters that concern us, bring us in closer touch with Americans and speak for us in something like an official manner.

Some fault is found with us for sticking to our old customs here, especially in the matter of clothes, but the reason is that we find American clothes much inferior, so far as comfort and warmth go. The Chinaman's coat for the winter is very durable, very light and very warm. It is easy and not in the way. If he wants to work, he slips out of it in a moment and can put it on again as quickly. Our shoes and hats also are better, we think, for our purposes, than the American clothes. Most of us have tried the American clothes, and they make us feel as if we were in the stocks.

I have found out, during my residence in this country, that much of the Chinese prejudice against Americans is unfounded, and I no longer put faith in the wild tales that were told about them in our village, though some of the Chinese, who have been here twenty years and who are learned men, still believe that there is no marriage in this country, that the land is infested with demons, and that all the people are given

"How Can America Be My Home?" by Lee Chew, continued

over to general wickedness. I know better. Americans are not all bad, nor are they wicked wizards. Still, they have their faults, and their treatment of us is outrageous.

The reason why so many Chinese go into the laundry business in this country is because it requires little capital and is one of the few opportunities that are open. Men of other nationalities who are jealous of the Chinese, because he is a more faithful worker than one of their people, have raised such a great outcry about Chinese cheap labor that they have shut him out of working on farms or in factories or building railroads or making streets or digging sewers. He cannot practice any trade, and his opportunities to do business are limited to his own countrymen. So he opens a laundry when he quits domestic service.

Stop and Record
Make some notes in the "Body" section of the Outline (page 63).

The treatment of the Chinese in this country is all wrong and mean. It is persisted in merely because China is not a fighting nation. The Americans would not dare to treat Germans, English, Italians, or even Japanese as they treat the Chinese, because if they did there would be a war.

There is no reason for the prejudice against the Chinese. The cheap labor cry was always a falsehood. Their labor was never cheap, and is not cheap now. It has always commanded the highest market price. But the trouble is that the Chinese are such excellent and faithful workers that bosses will have no others when they can get them. If you look at men working on the street, you will find an overseer for every four or five of them. That watching is not necessary for Chinese. They work as well when left to themselves as they do when someone is looking at them. . . .

More than half the Chinese in this country would become citizens if allowed to do so, and would be patriotic Americans. But how can they make this country their home as matters now are! They are not allowed to bring wives here from China, and if they marry American women there is a great outcry.

All Congressmen acknowledge the injustice of the treatment of my people, yet they continue it. They have no backbone.

Under the circumstances, how can I call this my home, and how can anyone blame me if I take my money and go back to my village in China?

Stop and Record
Make some notes in the "Conclusion" section of the Outline (page 63).

Using the Strategy

To complete your outline, you must understand the writer's thesis. Try using this formula:

subject + how the author feels about the subject = the author's thesis

Directions: Write the thesis of "How Can America Be My Home?"

.... + ...

subject   how the author feels

= ....

thesis

Nonfiction

Understanding How Essays Are Organized

Understanding how an essay is organized can make it easier for you to find the thesis. You may have noticed that many essays have the same organizational pattern.

• **Use your Outline to organize the main idea and details of the essay.**

Directions: Review the Main Idea Organizer on page 182 of your handbook. Then write Chew's main idea and his supporting details on this Main Idea Organizer.

◀ **Main Idea Organizer**

Subject:		
Main Idea:		
Detail	**Detail**	**Detail**

E Connect

Making personal connections to a subject and message of an essay can help you meet your reading purpose.

- **Connect to an essay by recording your thoughts and feelings about the subject.**

Directions: Write how you would feel if you were treated as Lee Chew was.

....

....

....

After Reading

When you finish reading, take the time to consider what you did and did not understand about the essay.

F Pause and Reflect

Think back to your reading purpose and decide whether or not you understand the subject and thesis.

- **After you finish an essay, ask yourself, "How well did I meet my purpose?"**

Directions: Answer these questions about "How Can America Be My Home?"

What is the subject of the essay? ....

....

What is the author's main point? ....

....

How do you feel about the author's message? ....

....

Would you say you've met your reading purpose? Why or why not? ....

....

Reread

Use the strategy of questioning the author if you're not 100 percent certain you've met your purpose. Zero in on the parts you're unsure of. Then ask a few questions about these parts. Imagine the author is sitting right there next to you.

• **A powerful rereading strategy to use is questioning the author.**

Directions: Write three questions for Lee Chew. Then write what you imagine his answers would be.

Question #1 ....

....

....

Chew's answer: ....

....

....

Question #2 ....

....

....

Chew's answer: ....

....

....

Question #3 ....

....

....

Chew's answer: ....

....

Remember

Good readers retain the most important parts of an essay. Putting what the author has said into your own words can help.

• **Writing a summary can help you remember what you've read.**

Directions: Write a summary of "How Can America Be My Home?" Put Lee Chew's message into your own words. Then explain how the writing made you feel.

Summary

My Summary of "How Can America Be My Home?"

Reading a Biography

In a biography, a writer tells the story of someone's life. Most biographers have two goals in mind when writing:

1. They want to tell an interesting story about the events of a person's life.

2. They want to create a "portrait," or impression, of that person so that readers can understand what he or she was like.

Before Reading

When you read a biography, your job is to learn about the biographical subject's life and form your own impression of him or her. Practice using the reading process and the strategy of looking for cause and effect with this excerpt from a biography that tells the story of Queen Isabella of Spain.

A Set a Purpose

Your purpose is to find out as much as you can about the biographical subject, including what kind of life the person had and what he or she was really like.

• **To set your purpose, ask a question about the biographical subject.**

Directions: Write your purpose for reading the Queen Isabella biography here.

My purpose: ....

....

....

....

....

....

B Preview

After you set your purpose, preview the text. First, recall what you already know about the subject. Then take a quick look at the book's title, front and back covers, and table of contents.

Directions: Write what you already know about royalty, Spain, or Queen Isabella in particular. Then make some preview notes.

What I already know: ....

....

....

....

Preview Notes

What is the title of the biography?

Who is the author?

What did you learn from the front and back covers?

What did you learn from the table of contents?

Back Cover

Queen Isabella of Spain (1451–1504) is one of the most extraordinary monarchs of all time. During her reign, she and her husband, King Ferdinand of Aragon, made decisions that would change the course of history.

This book tells the story of Isabella's childhood, her romance with Ferdinand, and her reign as queen of one of the most powerful kingdoms of its day. This is the story of two Isabellas—Isabella the woman, who suffered unimaginable personal losses in her life, and Isabella the monarch, who wreaked unimaginable havoc on her people.

Hated by many, but admired by all, Isabella was "stronger than a strong man, more constant than any human soul, a marvelous example of honesty and virtue."

Front Cover

Isabella of Spain

HER LIFE

BY Cristina Maria Bernal

Nonfiction

Table of Contents

Plan

Next make a plan. As you read, look for "life-shaping" events in the subject's life. These can help you understand the subject's personality.

• **Use the strategy of looking for cause and effect.**

A Cause-Effect Organizer like the one below is a good way to keep track of "life-shaping" events.

During Reading

Now do a careful reading of the excerpt. Watch for important events in Isabella's life.

D Read with a Purpose

Keep in mind your reading purpose. Remember that you want to find out about Isabella's life and what she was really like.

Directions: Fill out the Causes/Events side of this Cause-Effect Organizer as you read. You'll return to the Effect box later.

Cause-Effect Organizer

Causes/Events

Effect

Isabella was a

from *Isabella of Spain: Her Life* by Cristina Maria Bernal

Chapter 1
A Princess Is Born

Isabella was born in 1451, the daughter of Juan II, King of Castile, and his second wife, Isabel of Portugal. Although she had longed for a boy, Queen Isabel was happy with her little namesake and vowed to herself that the child would never want for a single thing for as long as she lived.

At her birth, Isabella was second in line for the crown of Castile. Her half-brother Enrique, King Juan's child by his first wife, was crown prince. Enrique, who was twenty-seven years Isabella's senior, doted on the pretty little princess and took pleasure in spoiling her with jewels and other treasures.

Isabella's first years were happy ones. She was cared for by a group of nurses and servants who were there to do her bidding night and day. Isabella's mother spent as much time as she could with the child, although her duties at the palace often kept her away from the nursery for long stretches of time. Isabella's father, King Juan, also spent time with his daughter and took particular pleasure in telling the little girl the stories he had heard as a child.

Stop and Record
What events have you read about so far?
Make notes on your Cause-Effect Organizer (page 74).

In 1454, however, Isabella's world changed forever. When she was just three years old, her father died and her mother became overwhelmed by grief. As was expected, Enrique took his place as King of Castile. Shortly after her father died, Isabella's mother went mad and was hidden away from the rest of the royal family. For months, Isabella cried herself to sleep and prayed for her mother's safe return. For the first time in her life, Isabella felt very alone.

It was during this sad period that several Franciscan monks were brought to the palace classrooms to meet young Isabella and begin her formal education. One young priest told Isabella stories of Joan of Arc, the young French girl who led her people into battle to free France from English invaders. Isabella was fascinated by the story of Joan and asked to hear it again and again. Although she was still quite young, Isabella understood how extraordinary it was for a woman to become as powerful as Joan.

Stop and Record
What information can you add to your Cause-Effect Organizer (page 74)?

Using the Strategy

Keep in mind that when you read a biography, you need to think about the "portrait" the writer has created. What kind of person is the subject? Is he or she strong or weak? Intelligent or stupid? Kind or unkind? These are the questions you should ask yourself as you read.

Directions: Return to the Effect side of the Cause-Effect Organizer on page 74. In the box, tell what you know about Isabella. Refer as needed to your preview and any notes you took during reading.

Understanding How Biographies Are Organized

Biographies are usually told in chronological order, beginning with the birth of the subject. Tracking the sequence of events in the subject's life can help you better see the portrait the writer has created.

Directions: Use this Timeline to show important events in Isabella's childhood. Put the events in chronological order.

Timeline

1451	1451	1454
• Isabella is born in 1451.		

E Connect

When you read a biography, think about your impression of the person described.

• **Record your own thoughts and feelings as you read.**

Directions: Tell how you feel about Isabella at this point. Then make a prediction about her life.

I feel

I predict

After Reading

After you finish reading a biography, consider what you've learned.

F Pause and Reflect

At this point, you'll want to return to your reading purpose. Ask yourself, "Can I name several important events in the subject's life?"

• **To reflect on your purpose, ask yourself questions about the subject's life and your impression of him or her.**

Directions: Complete this chart. If you have trouble, do some rereading.

Three important events in Isabella's life	What she was like as a child
1.	
2.	
3.	

Nonfiction

Reread

If you haven't yet formed an impression of the subject, you may need to do some rereading.

• **Use the strategy of outlining to get more from your rereading.**

Directions: Take another look at the excerpt. Make notes on this part of an Outline. First identify important events. Then add details about how the event affected Isabella's view of the world or her feelings about herself.

> **Outline**

> **Queen Isabella of Spain**
>
> **I. Early years**
>
>   **A. Important event**
>
>   **1. Detail**
>
>   **2. Detail**
>
>   **B. Important event**
>
>   **1. Detail**
>
>   **2. Detail**
>
>   **C. Important event**
>
>   **1. Detail**
>
>   **2. Detail**

H Remember

Do your best to remember the most important details of a biography.

• Use Study Cards to record what you learned.

Directions: Complete these Study Cards about Queen Isabella of Spain.
Write the most important details from her biography.

Study Cards

The first years of Queen Isabella of Spain

Isabella's early education

Nonfiction

Reading an Autobiography

In an autobiography, the writer tells the story of his or her life. Most autobiographers have these two purposes in mind:

1. They want to tell their life story in an interesting or dramatic way.

2. They want to create a self-portrait readers can relate to and admire.

Before Reading

Your job when reading an autobiography is to learn as much as you can about the author's life, and then respond to the self-portrait he or she has created. Use the reading process and strategy of synthesizing to help you read and respond to an excerpt from an autobiography.

A Set a Purpose

Consider these two questions as you read: "What kind of life did the autobiographer have?" and "How do I feel about this person?"

• **To set your purpose, ask two questions about the autobiographer.**

Directions: Write two questions about *Theodore Roosevelt: An Autobiography*. Finding answers to these questions will be your purpose for reading.

Question #1: ....

....

....

Question #2: ....

....

....

Preview

After you set your purpose, begin previewing.

Directions: Preview the front and back covers of *Theodore Roosevelt: An Autobiography*. Make notes.

Back Cover

Learn about the life and times of Teddy Roosevelt, one of America's most controversial — and loveable — presidents.

Teddy Roosevelt, the 26th President of the United States, took office with the promise of a "square deal" for every American.

Roosevelt made good on his promise — and then some. In his eight years as President, Roosevelt expanded the powers of the presidency, battled big business on behalf of American workers, and steered the country to a more active role in world politics, especially in Europe and Asia. Here is Roosevelt's own account of his joyful childhood in New York, his "rough-riding" years as a cowboy, and his eventual rise to worldwide fame as a man who would always "walk softly and carry a big stick."

Front Cover

Great Men and Women in
American History Series

THEODORE ROOSEVELT

AN AUTOBIOGRAPHY

BY Theodore Roosevelt

Nonfiction

Important details I noticed:

detail #1 ....

....

detail #2 ....

....

detail #3 ....

....

The title:

....

....

The author:

....

....

....

Plan

When you've finished previewing, make a reading plan that can help you meet your purpose. The strategy of synthesizing works well with autobiographies. Synthesizing is like gathering up the pieces of a puzzle and figuring out how they fit together.

• **Use the strategy of synthesizing to help you see the "full picture" the autobiographer presents.**

During Reading

Now do a careful reading of the excerpt from Theodore Roosevelt's story of his life. Make notes as you go.

Directions: Record your notes during reading on this Key Topic Organizer. First, read the key topics in the left column. Write notes from the text that relate to the topics in the right column.

Key Topic Organizer

Key Topics	Notes from Reading
childhood	
family	
school	
travel	

D Read with a Purpose

Keep your purpose in mind as you read and make notes. Remember that you are looking for information about Roosevelt's life. You also want to form an *impression* of him.

from *Theodore Roosevelt: An Autobiography*

. . . The summers we spent in the country, now at one place, now at another. We children, of course, loved the country beyond anything. We disliked the city. We were always wildly eager to get to the country when spring came, and very sad when in the late fall the family moved back to town. In the country we of course had all kinds of pets—cats, dogs, rabbits, a coon, and a sorrel Shetland pony named General Grant. When my younger sister first heard of the real General Grant, by the way, she was much struck by the coincidence that someone should have given him the same name as the pony. (Thirty years later my own children had [their] pony Grant.) In the country we children ran barefoot much of the time, and the seasons went by in a round of uninterrupted and enthralling pleasures—supervising the haying and harvesting, picking apples, hunting frogs successfully and woodchucks unsuccessfully, gathering hickory-nuts and chestnuts for sale to patient parents, . . .

Stop and Record

Make notes about Roosevelt's childhood on your Key Topic Organizer (page 82). What interested him?

My father, Theodore Roosevelt, was the best man I ever knew. He combined strength and courage with gentleness, tenderness, and great unselfishness. He would not tolerate in us children selfishness or cruelty, idleness, cowardice, or untruthfulness. As we grew older he made us understand that the same standard of clean living was demanded for the boys as for the girls; that what was wrong in a woman could not be right in a man. With great love and patience, and the most understanding sympathy and consideration, he combined insistence on discipline. He never physically punished me but once, but he was the only man of whom I was ever really afraid. I do not mean that it was a wrong fear, for he was entirely just, and we children adored him. We used to wait in the library in the evening until we could hear his key rattling in the latch of the front hall, and then rush out to greet him; and we would troop into his room while he was dressing, to stay there as long as we were permitted, eagerly examining anything which came out of his pockets which could be regarded as an attractive novelty. Every child has fixed in his memory various details which strike it as of grave

from _Theodore Roosevelt: An Autobiography,_ continued

importance. The trinkets he used to keep in a little box on his dressing-table we children always used to speak of as "treasures." The word, and some of the trinkets themselves, passed on to the next generation. My own children, when small, used to troop into my room while I was dressing, and the gradually accumulating trinkets in the "ditty-box"—the gift of an enlisted man in the navy— always excited rapturous joy. On occasions of solemn festivity each child would receive a trinket for his or her "very own." My children, by the way, enjoyed one pleasure I do not remember enjoying myself. When I came back from riding, the child who brought the bootjack would itself promptly get into the boots, and clump up and down the room with a delightful feeling of kinship with Jack of the seven-league strides.

The punishing incident I have referred to happened when I was four years old. I bit my elder sister's arm. I do not remember biting her arm, but I do remember running down to the yard, perfectly conscious that I had committed a crime. From the yard I went into the kitchen, got some dough from the cook, and crawled under the kitchen table. In a minute or two my father entered from the yard and asked where I was. The warm-hearted Irish cook had a characteristic contempt for "informers," but although she said nothing she compromised between informing and her conscience by casting a look under the table. My father immediately dropped on all fours and darted for me. I feebly heaved the dough at him, and, having the advantage of him because I could stand up under the table, got a fair start for the stairs, but was caught halfway up them. The punishment that ensued fitted the crime, and I hope—and believe—that it did me good. . . .

I was a sickly, delicate boy, suffered much from asthma, and frequently had to be taken away on trips to find a place where I could breathe. One of my memories is of my father walking up and down the room with me in his arms at night when I was a very small person, and of sitting up in bed gasping, with my father and mother trying to help me. I went very little to school. I never went to the public schools, as my own children later did, both at the "Cove School" at Oyster Bay and at the "Ford School" in Washington. For a few months I attended Professor McMullen's school on Twentieth Street near the house where I was born, but most of the time I had tutors. As I have already said, my aunt taught me when I was small. At one time we had a French governess, a loved and valued "mam'selle," in the household.

Stop and Record

Make notes about Roosevelt's family and schooling on your Key Topic Organizer (page 82). What was Roosevelt's early life like?

Reading an Autobiography ■

NAME .... FOR USE WITH PAGES 204–217

from *Theodore Roosevelt: An Autobiography,* continued

When I was ten years old I made my first journey to Europe. My birthday was spent in Cologne, and in order to give me a thoroughly "party" feeling I remember that my mother put on full dress for my birthday dinner. I do not think I gained anything from this particular trip abroad. I cordially hated it, as did my younger brother and sister. Practically all the enjoyment we had was in exploring any ruins or mountains when we could get away from our elders, and in playing in the different hotels. Our one desire was to get back to America, and we regarded Europe with the most ignorant chauvinism and contempt. Four years later, however, I made another journey to Europe, and was old enough to enjoy it thoroughly and profit by it.

While still a small boy I began to take an interest in natural history. I remember distinctly the first day that I started on my career as zoologist. I was walking up Broadway, and as I passed the market to which I used sometimes to be sent before breakfast to get strawberries I suddenly saw a dead seal laid out on a slab of wood. That seal filled me with every possible feeling of romance and adventure. I asked where it was killed, and was informed in the harbor. I had already begun to read some of Mayne Reid's books and other boys' books of adventure, and I felt that this seal brought all these adventures in realistic fashion before me. As long as that seal remained there I haunted the neighborhood of the market day after day. I measured it, and I recall that, not having a tape measure, I had to do my best to get its girth with a folding pocket foot-rule, a difficult undertaking. I carefully made a record of the utterly useless measurements, and at once began to write a natural history of my own, on the strength of that seal. . . .

When I was fourteen years old, in the winter of '72 and '73, I visited Europe for the second time, and this trip formed a really useful part of my education. We went to Egypt, journeyed up the Nile, traveled through the Holy Land and part of Syria, visited Greece and Constantinople; and then we children spent the summer with a German family in Dresden. My first real collecting as a student of natural history was done in Egypt during this journey. By this time I had a good working knowledge of American bird life from the superficially scientific standpoint. I had no knowledge of the ornithology of Egypt, but I picked up in Cairo a book by an English clergyman, whose name I have now forgotten, who described a trip up the Nile, and in an appendix to his volume gave an account of his bird collection. I wish I could remember the name of the author now, for I owe that book very much. Without it I should have been collecting entirely in the dark, whereas with its aid I could generally find out what the birds were.

Stop and Record

Make notes on your Key Topic Organizer (page 82). What part did travel play in Teddy Roosevelt's growing-up years?

Using the Strategy

When you synthesize, you examine individual topics or ideas in a reading and then see how they all work together.

- **Use a Character Trait Web to help you zero in on one or two key topics.**

Directions: Complete a Character Trait Web about Theodore Roosevelt. Write traits in the rounded boxes. Then record one or more details from the text as proof for each trait.

Character Trait Web

Trait:

fun-loving

Proof: enjoyed pets

Proof: played games

Theodore Roosevelt

Trait:

Trait:

Proof:

Proof:

Proof:

Proof:

Understanding How
Autobiographies Are Organized

Most autobiographers tell their life story in chronological, or time, order.
They begin with birth or childhood and move forward from there.
Use a Timeline to track the events the writer describes.

Directions: Complete this Timeline. Write a note about what happened
for each age listed. You can also use information from the book cover.

Timeline

Age four	Age ten	Age fourteen

Nonfiction

Connect

Remember that a part of your purpose is to form an *impression* of the autobiographer. You can collect your feelings about the author on an Inference Chart.

- **Each time you form an impression of the autobiographer, you make a connection to the text.**

Directions: Read the left column. Then record in the right column your impression, based on Roosevelt's words or actions.

Inference Chart

What Theodore Roosevelt did or said	My impression of him . . .
participated in games	
greatly admired his father	
"I bit my elder sister's arm."	
was sickly and delicate	

After Reading

At this point, you'll want to reflect carefully on the self-portrait the writer has created.

F Pause and Reflect

Take a moment to think about what you've learned.

• **After you finish reading, put together what you've learned about the autobiographer.**

Directions: Answer these three questions about Theodore Roosevelt. Refer to your notes as needed.

1. What were two important events in Roosevelt's childhood?

2. How did the events affect him?

3. What kind of person was Theodore Roosevelt? Explain.

Nonfiction

Reread

If your impression of Roosevelt is still not clear, you'll need to do some rereading. As you reread, watch for the events that shaped his personality.

• Use a Cause-Effect Organizer to track life-shaping events.

<u>Directions:</u> List events from Roosevelt's childhood that may have had an effect on his personality, as described under "Effect" on the right.

◄ Cause-Effect Organizer ▶

Causes

had many pets

Effect

became a strong President,
known for a love of nature
and a fascination with the
politics of Europe and Asia

 Remember

It's important to remember your general impression of the autobiographer.

• Writing your opinion of the autobiographer can help you retain what you've learned.

<u>Directions:</u> Write your opinion of Theodore Roosevelt here. Then explain.

Here's how I feel about Roosevelt after reading this excerpt from his

autobiography:

....

....

....

Reading a Newspaper Article

You can learn what's happening around the world and in your community by reading a newspaper.

Before Reading

Use the reading process and the strategy of reading critically to help you read and understand a newspaper article about the sinking of the *Titanic*.

A Set a Purpose

Your general purpose for reading a newspaper article is to find out what it's about.

• **To set your purpose, take several words from the headline and use them in a question.**

Directions: Write your purpose for reading "San Francisco's Assessor Tells Story of the Wreck of the *Titanic*" below. Then write some prereading questions about the article.

My purpose: ....

....

....

....

My questions: ....

....

....

....

....

....

....

Nonfiction

NAME ....

FOR USE WITH PAGES 218–233

B Preview

The lead, or first few paragraphs, of a newspaper article usually tells *who, what, where, when,* and *why.*

__Directions:__ Read the headline and first paragraphs of the article that follows. Then complete as much of this 5 W's Organizer as you can.

◀ **5 W's Organizer**

Subject

Who	What	Where	When	Why

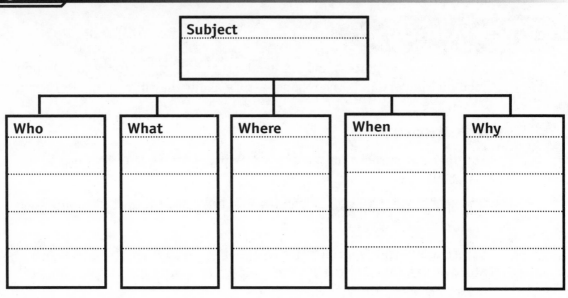

THE BULLETIN SAN FRANCISCO

April 19, 1912

San Francisco's Assessor Tells Story of the Wreck of the Titanic from Which He Escapes After Thrilling Experience

NEW YORK, April 19. — Dr. Washington Dodge of San Francisco, at the Hotel Wolcott here, gave the following account of the wreck:

"We had retired to our stateroom, and the noise of the collision was not at all alarming. We had just fallen asleep. My wife awakened me and said that something had happened to the ship. We went on deck and everything seemed quiet and orderly.

"The orchestra was playing a lively tune. They started to lower the lifeboats after a lapse of some minutes. There was little excitement."

Plan

Next make a plan. Choose a reading strategy that can help you understand and evaluate the article.

• **Use the strategy of reading critically with newspaper articles.**

Directions: Make notes on this Critical Reading Chart as you read the *Titanic* article.

Critical Reading Chart

Questions	My Notes
What facts are presented?	
What opinions are presented?	
Are the sources authoritative and reliable?	
Is the evidence convincing?	
Is there another side of the story?	

Nonfiction

During Reading

Now do a careful reading of the article.

D   Read with a Purpose

Keep in mind your reading purpose. Use your Critical Reading Chart to help you separate facts from opinions.

"San Francisco's Assessor Tells Story of the Wreck of the *Titanic,*" continued

SHIP SEEMED SAFER

"As the lifeboats were being launched, many of the first-cabin passengers expressed their preference of staying on the ship. The passengers were constantly being assured that there was no danger, but that as a matter of extra precaution the women and children should be placed in the lifeboats.

"Everything was still quiet and orderly when I placed Mrs. Dodge and the boy in the fourth or fifth boat. I believe there were 20 boats lowered away altogether. I did what I could to help in keeping order, as after the sixth or seventh boat was launched the excitement began.

"Some of the passengers fought with such desperation to get into the lifeboats that the officers shot them, and their bodies fell into the ocean.

"It was 10:30 when the collision occurred, and 1:55 o'clock when the ship went down," he said. "The major stood with John Jacob Astor as the water rolled over the *Titanic.*"

Stop and Record

What facts about the sinking of the Titanic does Dodge present? Record them on your Critical Reading Chart (page 93).

CAPTAIN WAS CALM

"I saw Colonel Astor, the major, and Captain Smith standing together about 11:30 o'clock. There was absolutely no excitement among them. Captain Smith said there was no danger.

"The starboard side of the *Titanic* struck the big berg and the ice was piled up on the deck. None of us had the slightest realization

> **"San Francisco's Assessor Tells Story of the Wreck of the *Titanic*," continued**

that the ship had received its death wound.

"Mrs. [Isidor] Straus showed most admirable heroism. She refused in a very determined manner to leave her husband, although she was twice entreated to get into the boats. Straus declined with great force to get in the boat while any women were left.

"I wish you would say for me that Colonel Astor, the major, Captain Smith, and every man in the cabins acted the part of a hero in that awful night.

"As the excitement began I saw an officer of the *Titanic* shoot down two steerage passengers who were endeavoring to rush the lifeboats. I have learned since that twelve of the steerage passengers were shot altogether, one officer shooting down six. The first-cabin men and women behaved with great heroism."

Stop and Record

What opinions about the sinking of the Titanic does Dodge present? Record them on your Critical Reading Chart (page 93). Show what evidence, if any, he provides.

OWES LIFE TO STEWARD

One of the stewards of the *Titanic*, with whom Mr. and Mrs. Dodge had crossed the Atlantic before on the *Olympic*, knew them well. He recognized Dodge as the thirteenth boat was being filled. The steerage passengers were being shot down and some of the steerage passengers were stabbing right and left in an endeavor to reach the boat.

The thirteenth boat was filled on one side with children, fully 20 or 30 of them, and a few women. All in the boat were panic-stricken and screaming. The steward had been ordered to take charge of the thirteenth, and, seizing Dodge, pushed him into the boat, exclaiming that he needed his help in caring for his helpless charges.

Dodge said that when the boats were drawing away from the ship they could hear the orchestra playing "Lead, Kindly Light," and rockets were going up from the *Titanic* in the wonderfully clear night. "We could see from the distance that two boats were being made ready to be lowered. The panic was in the steerage, and it was that portion of the ship that the shooting was made necessary."

"I will never forget," Mrs. Dodge said, "the awful scene of the great steamer as we drew away. From the upper rails heroic husbands and fathers were waving and throwing kisses to their womenfolk in the receding lifeboats."

Stop and Record

What does Mrs. Dodge report about the Titanic disaster? Record her opinion on your Critical Reading Chart (page 93).

Nonfiction

Using the Strategy

To read critically, you must look for the writer's opinion and the way the writer supports the position. Note if the writer considers other viewpoints.

• **Use an Argument Chart to examine and analyze a newspaper article.**

Directions: Add notes about the writer's support for the viewpoint shown and an opposing viewpoint. Then write another viewpoint stated by Dodge, along with notes to support the viewpoint and an opposite viewpoint.

Argument Chart

Viewpoint	Support	Opposing Viewpoint
"Mrs. [Isidor] Straus showed most admirable heroism."		

Understanding How
Newspaper Articles Are Organized

Most newspaper articles follow a standard organization called an *inverted pyramid*. See page 229 of the *Reader's Handbook* for details.

Directions: First review the 5 W's Organizer on page 92 that you began after reading the lead. Add any new details. Then show the organization of the article about the wreck of the *Titanic* on the inverted pyramid.

Inverted Pyramid

Most important details:

Detail #1

Detail #2

Less important details:

Detail #3

Detail #4

Least important details:

Detail #5

Nonfiction

Connect

Making a connection means reacting to specific facts and details in the article.

- **One way to make a connection is to record how the newspaper article made you feel.**

The article about the *Titanic* disaster made me feel _____ because _____

....

....

....

....

....

After Reading

After reading, think about what you learned.

 Pause and Reflect

As you reflect, consider whether you've met your reading purpose.

- **Ask yourself some questions about the article you just finished.**

Directions: Complete this reading checklist.

Reading Checklist	Yes	No
I can state Dodge's opinion in my own words.		
I understand how the article is organized.		
I can answer <u>who</u>, <u>what</u>, <u>where</u>, <u>when</u>, and <u>why</u> questions.		
I understand Dodge's evidence and have decided how reliable it is.		

NAME

 Reread

If you feel you haven't learned the facts of the article well enough, you'll need to do some rereading.

• **Use the strategy of summarizing when you reread.**

Directions: Make Summary Notes about the *Titanic* newspaper account.

◄ Summary Notes

Article headline:

Subject:

Author's viewpoint:

Detail #1

Detail #2

Detail #3

Detail #4

Detail #5

Detail #6

Nonfiction

Remember

If you can remember the most important details of an article, you can speak knowledgeably about the subject later. One option is to write your thoughts in a journal. The act of putting down your thoughts in writing will help the article stick in your mind.

• **Writing a journal entry can help you remember an article.**

Directions: Write a brief journal entry about "San Francisco's Assessor Tells Story of the Wreck of the *Titanic*."

Journal Entry

Reading a Magazine Article

If your assignment is to read and respond to a magazine article, which tools and strategies should you use, and how should you use them? Practice here.

Before Reading

Use the reading process and the strategy of questioning the author to help you read and respond to a magazine travel article about an ancient Inca city.

A Set a Purpose

Before reading, decide on a purpose. Ask yourself, "What do I hope to learn from the article?"

- **Use key words from the title of the article to form a reading purpose question.**

Directions: Write your purpose for reading a magazine article called "Journey to a Secret City." Then predict what you think the article is about.

My purpose: ....

....

My predictions: ....

....

....

B Preview

When you preview, look for clues about the **subject** of the article. Pay attention to the title, any photographs or illustrations, headings or large type, and the first paragraph.

Nonfiction

Directions: Preview "Journey to a Secret City." Write your preview notes below.

The title: ....

What I noticed about the art: ....

What I learned from the headings: ....

What I learned from the first paragraph: ....

....

JOURNEY TO A SECRET CITY

by Martha O'Brien

Last year, I took a journey to one of the most breathtaking places on earth: Machu Picchu, Peru. I describe Machu Picchu as breathtaking with some knowledge of the world. I've hiked the Appalachian Trail, shopped for scarves in Istanbul, bicycled in the Loire Valley, and stood small at the base of Mount Fuji. But Machu Picchu—it tops them all. Truly, this place is heaven on earth.

Machu Picchu is an ancient Inca city, located about 50 miles northwest of the Peruvian city of Cuzco. It is perched high upon a rock in a narrow saddle between two craggy mountain peaks, and overlooks the twisting Urubamba River 2,000 feet below.

Stop and Record
What is the subject of this article? Write your answer to the first question under Questions and Answers (page 105).

"Journey to a Secret City" by Martha O'Brien, continued

Journey Begins in Cuzco

As many travelers can attest, journeying to Machu Picchu is no walk in the park. My trip began in Cuzco, a small city on the eastern slope of the Andes Mountain Range. Cuzco, which the Indians call the center of the world, is the former imperial capital of the Incas.

Our train to Machu Picchu left the small Cuzco station at sunrise so as to beat the suffocating late morning Peruvian heat. After four hours' travel through one of the most spectacular stretches in the world, we arrived at the foot of the mountain Machu Picchu.

Our guide, ever patient with his camera-toting charges, helped us from the train and onto a rickety bus that jerked and honked its way up the mountain at breakneck speed. Our destination was the secret city, and the bus driver was determined to make it in record time.

The Lost City

An hour later, we pulled to a stop outside the Machu Picchu Ruinas hotel. The guide, who showed no signs of the altitude sickness that was afflicting us all, opened his arms and said with a broad grin, "Welcome to the lost city of Machu Picchu, the most spectacular place on earth." What we took to be exaggeration turned out to be the absolute truth.

Stop and Question

How do you think the author feels about Machu Picchu? Answer the second question under Questions and Answers on (page 105).

Stretched before us was imposing Machu Picchu, which is thought to be one of the largest pre-Columbian sites ever discovered intact. Machu Picchu, built high into the clouds at 7,700 feet, spreads over five square miles, with over 3,000 steps linking its many different levels. Archeological and historical evidence indicates that it was once the mountain retreat of the Inca leader Pachacuti Yupanqui, who ruled from c. 1438–1471. Historians have also suggested that it may have been a religious

Nonfiction

sanctuary, or temple, inhabited by priests and "Virgins of the Sun." Excavation has turned up 135 skeletons, 109 of which were women.

Rediscovery by an Explorer

Our guide, of course, was eager to supply background information about Machu Picchu. From him we learned that the city was ignored and later forgotten by Spanish colonial authorities because of its abandoned condition. It was "rediscovered" in 1911 by an explorer named Hiram Bingham. Bingham's well-known books, *Across South America* (1911) and *Lost City of the Incas* (1948), detail his expedition to Machu Picchu.

Close to 700,000 tourists a year visit Machu Picchu, although the Peruvian government has worked hard to maintain the aura of secrecy that surrounds the site. To those fortunate enough to make the journey to Machu Picchu, the words of the philosopher Napoleon Polo Casilla still ring true:

"To visit Machu Picchu, you must prepare the soul, sharpen the senses. Forget, for some minutes, the small and transcendental problems of our lives, of modern . . . man."

Stop and Question

What do you think the author wants to teach you about Machu Picchu? Write your answer to the third question under Questions and Answers (page 105).

C Plan

After your preview, make a reading plan. What strategy can help you find and understand the subject and main idea of this article?

- **Use the strategy of questioning the author to help you get *more* from a magazine article.**

Questioning the author involves thinking about the decisions the author made. It can help you spot the writer's most important details.

NAME ....

During Reading

Now go back and do a careful reading of "Journey to a Secret City." As you read, ask questions of the author. Write your answers below.

D Read with a Purpose

Keep in mind your purpose for reading. Remember that you're looking for information about the subject, how the author feels about the subject, and supporting details for the author's main idea.

Directions: Write answers to your author questions here. Then write your own question for the author.

Questions and Answers

1. What is the subject of the article?

....

....

2. How do you think the author feels about Machu Picchu?

....

....

3. What do you think the writer wants to teach you about Machu Picchu?

....

....

4. Your question for the author:

....

....

....

Nonfiction

Using the Strategy

One of the reasons you question an author is to find out the main idea of the article.

- **Use a Main Idea Organizer to keep track of important information.**

Main Idea Organizer

Subject: Machu Picchu

Main Idea:

Detail #1:	Detail #2:	Detail #3:

Understanding How Magazine Articles Are Organized

Good magazine writers answer the 5 W's in their writing.

Directions: Write the most important details of the article on this organizer.

5 W's Organizer

Subject				

Who	What	Where	When	Why

Nonfiction

Connect

Record your personal reactions to a magazine article as you read.
Make additional comments later, after you finish.

- **Recording your reactions can help you process and remember what you've learned.**

Directions: Circle *interesting* or *not interesting*. Then tell what you want to learn more about.

I thought the article was interesting / not interesting because ....

....

....

Here's what I'd like to find out more about: ....

....

....

After Reading

After you finish reading, decide whether or not you agree with the author's main idea.

Pause and Reflect

Begin by reflecting on your purpose.

- **To reflect on your purpose, ask yourself, "Have I accomplished what I set out to do?"**

Directions: Check *yes* or *no* to the items on this list.

Checklist	Yes	No
I understand the topic of the article.		
I understand the author's main idea.		
I can restate the main idea in my own words.		

Reread

Most often writers present a viewpoint in the hopes of convincing you to adopt the same position. At this point, think about the author's viewpoints.

- **Use the strategy of reading critically to evaluate the viewpoint and evidence presented.**

Directions: Answer the five questions in the Critical Reading Chart.

Critical Reading Chart

My Questions	My Answers
1. Is the main idea or viewpoint clear?	
2. What evidence is presented?	
3. Are the sources authoritative and reliable?	
4. Is the evidence convincing?	
5. Is there another side to the story?	

Nonfiction

H Remember

Using the information you've read can help you remember it.

- **To remember a magazine article, tell it to a friend or write a journal entry.**

Directions: Write your thoughts and ideas about "Journey to a Secret City" in a journal entry. Tell what the article was about and how it made you feel.

Journal Entry

NAME ....

FOR USE WITH PAGES 247–255

Focus on Persuasive Writing

Persuasive writing makes an argument. Your job is to understand and evaluate the argument the writer presents. This three-step plan can help.

Step 1: Find the topic and viewpoint.

The **topic** is the subject of the writing. The **viewpoint** is the author's opinion about the subject.

Directions: Read the following newspaper editorial. Circle the topic. Write the viewpoint in the margin.

Editorial Page

Helmets Save Lives

This year alone, more than four hundred children were injured while riding skateboards and scooters. The most serious of these injuries involved some kind of head trauma. Doctors believe that many of these injuries could have been prevented had the riders been wearing helmets. But since our state has no helmet law for scooter and skateboard riders, most of our children never put helmets on their heads.

This month, our state legislature is considering a law that would make helmet use mandatory for scooter and skateboard riders under the age of eighteen. This law would be similar to the bike helmet law that has been on the books for three years.

Some parents and children have been very vocal in their fight against helmet laws. Parents say helmets are a waste of money and a source of family arguments. Kids say they are embarrassing.

But statistics show that children who wear helmets have far fewer injuries than children who do not. More remarkable is the fact that children who wear helmets rarely sustain head injuries at all.

Children are dying from scooter and skateboard injuries in our state. Helmets save lives. Which part of this equation do parents and lawmakers have trouble understanding? Write to your district representative today to express your support of the new helmet law.

Nonfiction

Step 2: Locate support for the viewpoint.

Good persuasive writers support their viewpoint with convincing facts, details, and examples.

Directions: Reread the editorial. Underline support for the writer's viewpoint.

Step 3: Evaluate the argument.

After you finish reading, evaluate the viewpoint, support, and opposing viewpoint. Then decide how you feel about the writer's argument.

Directions: Complete this Argument Chart. Write the author's viewpoint and support. Then, describe the opposing viewpoint.

Argument Chart

Viewpoint	Support	Opposing Viewpoint
Here's how I feel about the argument:	The argument is / is not effective.	Here's why:

Write the author's viewpoint here.

List the support for the viewpoint here.

Write your ideas about the other side of the argument here.

NAME ....

FOR USE WITH PAGES 256–264

Focus on Speeches

The reading process can help you understand and evaluate a speaker's message. Follow these steps.

Step 1: Look for the 5 W's.

On your first reading, look for *when*, *where*, and *why* the speech was given. Think about *what* the subject is, *who* gave the speech, and *who* the audience was.

Directions: Read the background information and beginning of John Brown's speech. Then complete the 5 W's Organizer.

John Brown's Final Address to the Court

In October of 1859, John Brown led a party of 18 men to Harpers Ferry, Virginia, hoping to incite an uprising of slaves in the area. The raiders were quickly captured and brought to trial for treason. Brown was hanged in Virginia on December 2, 1859. This speech was his final address to the court that convicted him.

I have, may it please the court, a few words to say.

In the first place, I deny everything but what I have all along admitted: of a design on my part to free slaves. I intended certainly to have made a clean thing of that matter, as I did last winter, when I went into Missouri and there took slaves without the snapping of a gun on either side, moving them through the country, and finally leaving them in Canada. I designed to have done the same thing again on a larger scale. That was all I intended. I never did intend murder, or treason, or the destruction of property, or to excite or incite slaves to rebellion, or to make insurrection.

I have another objection, and that is that it is unjust that I should suffer such a penalty. Had I interfered in the manner which I admit, and which I admit has been fairly proved—for I admire the truthfulness and candor of the greater portion of the witnesses who have testified in this case—had I so interfered in behalf of the rich, the powerful, the intelligent, the so-called great, or in the behalf of any of their friends, either father, mother, brother, sister, wife, or children, or any of that class, and suffered and sacrificed what I have in this interference, it would have been all right. Every man in this court would have deemed it an act worthy of reward rather than punishment.

5 W's Organizer

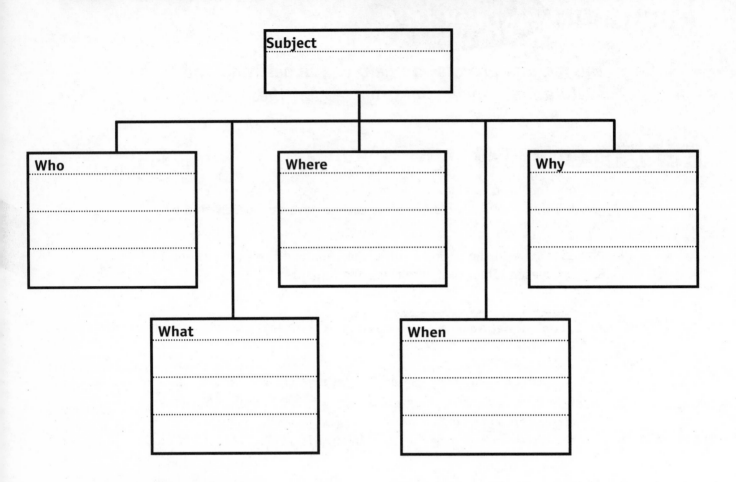

Step 2: Decide on the speaker's viewpoint.

Next, think about the speaker's viewpoint.

Directions: Write what you think was John Brown's viewpoint on the lines below.

John Brown spoke to explain ....

....

....

....

NAME ....

Step 3: React to the speaker's message.

Understanding your emotional reaction to a speech can help you better understand the speaker's message.

Directions: Complete this chart. Refer to your notes as needed.

Brown's speech made me feel

This is what I'd like to say to John Brown:

Nonfiction

Focus on Real-world Writing

Real-world, or informational, writing can help you stay informed. Follow these steps.

Step 1: Identify your purpose.

First, figure out your purpose for reading.

Directions: Look at this flier for a school field trip.
What is your reading purpose?

My purpose:

IMPORTANT IMPORTANT IMPORTANT IMPORTANT

7th Grade Field Trip
Gettysburg, PA
Your Attendance
Is Required!

Trip date: Wednesday, May 1
Departure time: 6:30 A.M. sharp!
Meeting place: the school parking lot

What to Bring

Required items: Gettysburg packet from class, notebook and pencils, brown bag lunch

Optional items: camera, spending money for souvenirs, snacks for the bus ride

IMPORTANT IMPORTANT IMPORTANT IMPORTANT

Step 2: Find out what you need to know.

Pay attention to information that is important to you.

Directions: Highlight the most important points in the field trip flier.
Use the information to complete this web.

 Web

Step 3: Remember and use the information.

Decide how the information in the writing affects you personally. Then
figure out a way to remember it.

Directions: Write
information about the
field trip on this
calendar page. Include
the most important
details.

Wednesday, May

1

Memo:

Reading a Short Story

Short stories can be funny, serious, weird, spooky, or just plain amazing. The key to reading them is asking— and answering—the right kinds of questions.

Before Reading

Practice asking and answering questions here. Use the reading process and the strategy of using graphic organizers to help you read and respond to a famous story by O. Henry.

A Set a Purpose

Setting your purpose first, before you begin reading, can help you get more from a short story.

• **To set your purpose, turn the title of the story into a question.**

Directions: Write your purpose for reading O. Henry's "After Twenty Years" below. Then predict what you think the story will be about.

My purpose: ....

....

My predictions: ....

....

....

B Preview

Always preview before you begin reading. Skim the background section and the first paragraph or two of the story. Highlight words and phrases you think are important.

Directions: Write your notes on this chart.

◀ **Preview Chart** ▶

Preview questions	My notes
What is the title of the story?	
Who is the author?	
What did you learn from the background section?	
What ideas did the first two paragraphs give you about the story?	
What repeated words did you see?	

Before You Read

What you need to know about "After Twenty Years" and O. Henry

THE SELECTION "After Twenty Years" was first published in 1906. In this work, O. Henry reflects his firmly held belief that crime doesn't pay.

THE AUTHOR O. Henry's real name was William Sidney Porter. Porter was born in 1862 in North Carolina. When he was thirty years old, he started a humorous weekly magazine called *The Rolling Stone*. To earn extra money, he took a job as a bank teller. Not long after, Porter was accused of stealing money from the bank. As a result, he spent three years in prison.

Porter's years in prison gave him material for dozens of short stories. Many of his characters are based on the inmates and guards he met while in jail. After he was set free, Porter changed his name to O. Henry, hoping to hide his past. Under this pen name, Porter published over sixty short stories before his death in 1910. Many say that he is the greatest short story writer in American history.

THE THEME Justice

LITERARY FOCUS Surprise endings

FURTHER READING "The Ransom of Red Chief" and "A Retrieved Reformation" by O. Henry

After Twenty Years
by O. Henry

THE POLICEMAN on the beat moved up the avenue impressively.

The impressiveness was habitual and not for show, for spectators were few. The time was barely 10 o'clock at night, but chilly gusts of wind with a taste of rain in them had well nigh depeopled the streets.

Trying doors as he went, twirling his club with many intricate and artful movements, turning now and then to cast his watchful eye down the pacific thoroughfare, the officer, with his stalwart form and slight swagger, made a fine picture of a guardian of the peace.

The vicinity was one that kept early hours. Now and then you might see the lights of a cigar store or of an all-night lunch counter; but the majority of the doors belonged to business places that had long since been closed.

When about midway of a certain block the policeman suddenly slowed his walk. In the doorway of a darkened hardware store a man leaned, with an unlighted cigar in his mouth.

As the policeman walked up to him, the man spoke up quickly. "It's all right, officer," he said, reassuringly. "I'm just waiting for a friend. It's an appointment made twenty years ago. Sounds a little funny to you, doesn't it? Well, I'll explain if you'd like to make certain it's all straight. About that long ago there used to be a restaurant where this store stands—'Big Joe' Brady's restaurant."

"Until five years ago," said the policeman. "It was torn down then."

The man in the doorway struck a match and lit his cigar. The light showed a pale, square-jawed face with keen eyes, and a little white scar near his right eyebrow. His scarf-pin was a large diamond, oddly set.

"Twenty years ago tonight," said the man, "I dined here at 'Big Joe' Brady's with Jimmy Wells, my best chum, and the finest chap in the world. He and I were raised here in New York, just like two brothers, together. I was eighteen and Jimmy was twenty. The next morning I was to start for the West to make my fortune. You couldn't have dragged Jimmy out of New York; he thought it was the only place on earth. Well, we agreed that night that we would meet here again exactly twenty years from that date and time, no matter what our conditions might be or from what distance we might have to come. We figured that in twenty years each of us ought to have our destiny worked out and our fortunes made, whatever they were going to be."

Stop and Record

Make some notes in the "Beginning" section of the Story Organizer (page 123). Tell what happens and who the characters are.

NAME

"It sounds pretty interesting," said the policeman. "Rather a long time between meets, though, it seems to me. Haven't you heard from your friend since you left?"

"Well, yes, for a time we corresponded," said the other. "But after a year or two we lost track of each other. You see, the West is a pretty big proposition, and I kept hustling around over it pretty lively. But I know Jimmy will meet me here if he's alive, for he always was the truest, staunchest old chap in the world. He'll never forget. I came a thousand miles to stand in this door tonight, and it's worth it if my old partner turns up."

The waiting man pulled out a handsome watch, the lids of it set with small diamonds.

"Three minutes to ten," he announced. "It was exactly ten-o'clock when we parted here at the restaurant door."

"Did pretty well out West, didn't you?" asked the policeman.

"You bet! I hope Jimmy has done half as well. He was a kind of plodder, though, good fellow as he was. I've had to compete with some of the sharpest wits going to get my pile. A man gets in a groove in New York. It takes the West to put a razor-edge on him."

The policeman twirled his club and took a step or two.

"I'll be on my way. Hope your friend comes around all right. Going to call time on him sharp?"

"I should say not!" said the other. "I'll give him half an hour at least. If Jimmy is alive on earth he'll be here by that time. So long, officer."

"Good night, sir," said the policeman, passing on along his beat, trying doors as he went.

There was now a fine, cold drizzle falling, and the wind had risen from its uncertain puffs into a steady blow. The few foot passengers astir in that quarter hurried dismally and silently along with coat collars turned high and pocketed hands. And in the door of the hardware store the man who had come a thousand miles to fill an appointment, uncertain almost to absurdity, with the friend of his youth, smoked his cigar and waited.

About twenty minutes he waited, and then a tall man in a long overcoat, with collar turned up to his ears, hurried across from the opposite side of the street. He went directly to the waiting man.

"Is that you, Bob?" he asked, doubtfully.

"Is that you, Jimmy Wells?" cried the man in the door.

"Bless my heart!" exclaimed the new arrival, grasping both the other's hands with his own. "It's Bob, sure as fate. I was certain I'd find you here if you were still in existence. Well, well, well! Twenty years is a long time. The old restaurant's gone, Bob; I wish it had lasted, so we could have had another dinner there. How has the West treated you, old man?"

"Bully; it has given me everything I asked it for. You've changed lots, Jimmy. I never thought you were so tall by two or three inches."

Fiction

"After Twenty Years" by O. Henry, continued

"Oh, I grew a bit after I was twenty."

"Doing well in New York, Jimmy?"

"Moderately. I have a position in one of the city departments. Come on, Bob; we'll go around to a place I know of, and have a good long talk about old times."

The two men started up the street arm in arm. The man from the West, his egotism enlarged by success, was beginning to outline the history of his career. The other, submerged in his overcoat, listened with interest.

Stop and Record
Make some notes in the "Middle" section of the Story Organizer (page 123).
What do you learn about the two friends?

At the corner stood a drug store, brilliant with electric light. When they came into this each of them turned simultaneously to gaze upon the other's face.

The man from the West stopped suddenly and released his arm. "You're not Jimmy Wells," he snapped. "Twenty years is a long time, but not long enough to change a man's nose from a Roman to a pug."

"It sometimes changes a man into a bad one," said the tall man. "You've been under arrest for ten minutes, 'Silky' Bob. Chicago thinks you may have dropped over our way and wires to us she wants to have a chat with you. Going quietly, are you? That's sensible. Now, before we go to the station here's a note I was asked to hand to you. You may read it here at the window. It's from Patrolman Wells."

The man from the West unfolded the little piece of paper handed him. His hand was steady when he began to read, but it trembled a little by the time he had finished. The note was rather short.

Bob:

I was at the appointed place on time. When you struck the match to light your cigar I saw it was the face of the man wanted in Chicago. Somehow I couldn't do it myself, so I went around and got a plain-clothes man to do the job.

—Jimmy

Stop and Record
Make some notes in the "End" section of the Story Organizer (page 123).
What happens to surprise you?

Plan

Next make a plan. What's the best way to meet your reading purpose? If your purpose is to find out what happens in the story, a graphic organizer can help.

• **Practice the strategy of using graphic organizers.**

During Reading

Now go back and do a careful reading of O. Henry's story. As you read, make notes on the organizer below. It can help you keep track of what happens in the story.

Read with a Purpose

Keep in mind your purpose as you read. Remember that you need to ask and answer questions about the story.

Directions: Make notes on this organizer as you read.

Story Organizer

Beginning	Middle	End
What happens?	What happens?	What happens?
Which characters are involved?	Which characters are involved?	Which characters are involved?

Fiction

Using the Strategy

All different kinds of graphic organizers work well with short stories. Choose the ones that work best for you.

• **A Fiction Organizer can help you keep track of important information about characters, setting, plot, theme, point of view, and style.**

Directions: Record what you know in this Fiction Organizer.

Fiction Organizer

Point of View	Characters	Setting

Title
"After Twenty Years" by O. Henry

Plot	Theme	Style

• **An Inference Chart works well when you have to interpret or make inferences about a character.**

Directions: Write what the character said or did in the left-hand column. Then write the inference you can make from those words or actions.

Inference Chart

What the characters say or do	What I can conclude about the character
Jimmy Wells	
"Silky Bob"	

Fiction

Understanding How Stories Are Organized

Short stories generally follow a pattern. You can map the organization of a story with a Plot Diagram similar to the one on page 309 of your handbook.

Directions: Use this Plot Diagram to show the organization of "After Twenty Years." Include the important details.

Plot Diagram

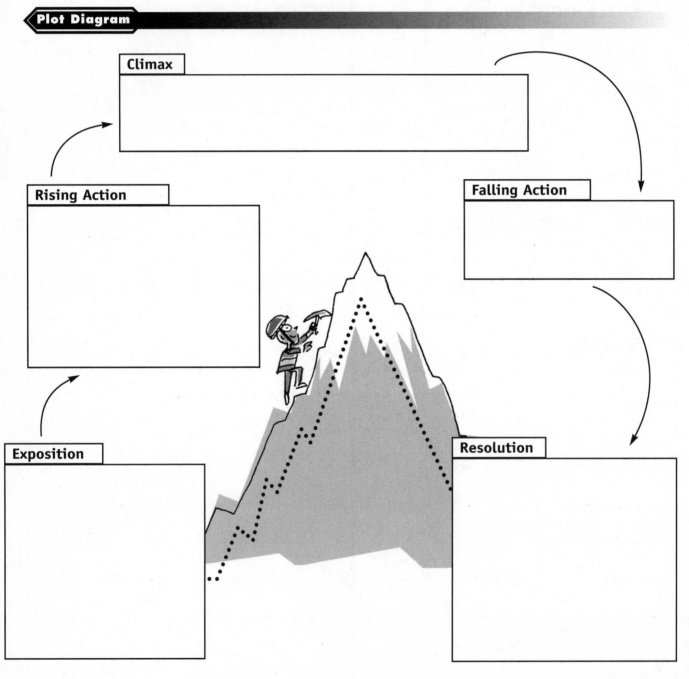

Climax

Rising Action

Falling Action

Exposition

Resolution

NAME ....

FOR USE WITH PAGES 294–314

E Connect

Reread the last few paragraphs of the story. Then record how the ending made you feel.

> • **Recording how a story made you feel can help you make a connection to the reading.**

The ending made me feel ....

....

....

....

....

After Reading

After reading most stories, you will be left with questions. The way to follow up on your questions is to go back through the story and look for answers.

Pause and Reflect

The surprise ending of "After Twenty Years" forces you to go back and look at the story again.

> • **After you finish a selection, ask yourself: "How well did I meet my purpose?"**

<u>**Directions:**</u> Explain how well you met your purpose here.

Comments about my purpose: ....

....

....

....

Reread

You can sharpen your thoughts about the ending and the story as a whole if you look back at the selection and do some rereading.

• **A powerful rereading strategy to use is close reading.**

Directions: Look at these lines from "After Twenty Years." Write what you learned from them on the chart.

Double-entry Journal

Text of "After Twenty Years"	What I Learned
"'You see, the West is a pretty big proposition, and I kept hustling around over it pretty lively.'"	
"'Did pretty well out West, didn't you?' asked the policeman."	
"'You've changed lots, Jimmy. I never thought you were so tall by two or three inches.'"	
"Somehow I couldn't do it myself, so I went around and got a plain-clothes man to do the job."	

 Remember

Good readers remember what they've read.

• **To remember a story, try making the information in the story your own.**

Directions: Write a journal entry about "After Twenty Years." Say what you did and didn't like about the selection, and support it with good details. Be sure to discuss the surprise ending.

Journal Entry

"After Twenty Years" by O. Henry

Reading a Novel

Reading a novel is like taking a journey. You'll discover some interesting people, places, and ideas. The key to enjoying the adventure is to stay focused and pay attention to what happens.

Before Reading

Practice reading and responding to a novel here. Use the reading process and the strategy of synthesizing to help you get more from Miguel de Cervantes's novel, *Don Quixote de la Mancha*.

 A Set a Purpose

When reading a novel for an assignment, your purpose is to understand major elements of the book, such as characters, setting, plot, and style.

• **To set your purpose, ask important questions about the major elements of the novel.**

Directions: You will be reading a selection from *Don Quixote de la Mancha*. What will be your purpose for reading? Write your questions about the major elements below.

Purpose Chart

Element	My Question
characters	Who are the major characters?
setting	
plot	
style	

Fiction

B Preview

Previewing a novel beforehand can help you know what to expect during your careful reading.

Directions: Preview the front and back covers. Check off each item as you preview.

Preview Checklist

- ☑ title
- ☑ author
- ☑ back cover
- ☑ information about the author

Back Cover

Meet the funny, adventurous, and valiant Don Quixote, who ranks as one of the most unforgettable literary characters of all time . . .

MIGUEL DE CERVANTES was born in 1547 in Alcalá, Spain. He was a novelist, poet, and playwright, and the creator of *Don Quixote de la Mancha,* a widely read classic of Western literature. Cervantes's novel is a humorous satire of chivalry and the romances popular at the time. It is also a love story between two unlikely characters: Don Quixote and his fascinating "lady," Dulcinea.

Don Quixote has played a significant role in the development of the modern novel. Cervantes's writing influenced many of the classic novelists of the 19th and 20th centuries, including Charles Dickens, Herman Melville, James Joyce, and Jorge Luis Borges.

Front Cover

A Classic Retelling of

DON QUIXOTE de la MANCHA

by Miguel de Cervantes

C Plan

After your preview, choose a strategy that can help you explore the elements of setting, characters, plot, and style.

- **Use the strategy of synthesizing to understand various literary elements and how they work together in a novel.**

When you synthesize, you look at a number of parts or elements individually and then put them together to see how they work with one another.

Directions: Make notes on this Fiction Organizer as you read the story of *Don Quixote*.

Fiction Organizer

Setting Where and when does the story take place?

Characters Who are they? What are they like?

Don Quixote de la Mancha

Plot What happens?

Style What is most memorable about the writing?

Fiction

During Reading

 D ## Read with a Purpose

Completing the Fiction Organizer as you read can help you stay focused on your purpose. Think about characters, setting, plot, and style.

Directions: Add notes to your organizer as you read.

---

from *Don Quixote de la Mancha* by Miguel de Cervantes

Once upon a time there lived in a small village in Spain called la Mancha a gentleman named Quixada or Queseda—historians do not agree about his exact name—whose house was full of all types of armor and weapons. This man, who was around fifty years old, had hard features and an old, withered face. At one time in his life, the man had been quite fond of hunting. But now, for a great portion of the year, he devoted himself to reading old books about the days of knighthood. He read these books with such keen delight that he forgot all about the pleasures of the hunt and neglected all his household duties as well. His interest in the days of knighthood grew to such a degree that he sold many acres of his lands in order to buy books that told of the adventures of the knights of old. He was certain that these books presented accurate histories of events that occurred in the days of chivalry.

Stop and Record

Make notes in the "Setting" section of the Fiction Organizer (page 131). Where and when does the story take place?

So eagerly did the man plunge into the readings of these books that he often spent whole days and nights poring over them; and so, in the end, because of little sleep and much reading, his brain became tired, and he came very close to losing his wits. All he could think of was the things he read about—enchantments, quarrels, battles, challenges, wounds, wooings, loves, tempests, and other impossible things, and those romantic tales so firmly took hold of him that he believed no history could be as true and sincere as they were.

Finally, with his wits almost gone, he was seized with one of the strangest ideas that a madman ever thought of, for it seemed to him right and necessary that he himself should become a knight errant and ride through the world in armor to seek adventures and experience for himself all that he had read about the knights of yore.

◄ **from *Don Quixote de la Mancha* by Miguel de Cervantes,** continued ►

Therefore, he decided that he would make a name for himself by righting the wrongs of the world and courting all kinds of dangers and difficulties, until in the end he should be rewarded for his bravery by the king of some mighty empire. So he pulled out the rusty armor that had belonged to his great-grandfather and had lain neglected in a forgotten corner of his house, and he scrubbed and polished it as best he could.

Now, a great necessity of any true knight was a trusty and noble horse on which to ride into battle and spirit away maidens who had been captured by dragons and such. So for this purpose, he called upon his own carriage horse, which, though bare-boned and ragged, seemed to him an excellent and noble steed. He spent four days inventing a name for his horse, saying to himself that it was only right that so famous a knight's horse, and so good a beast, should have a new and important sounding name that was worthy of his new position in life. Finally, having chosen and rejected all sorts of names, he hit upon the name Rocinante, which to him was perfect and sounded just right.

Because he had given his horse such a noble name, he made up his mind to give himself a name also, and so he spent another eight days wondering about that. Finally, he decided to call himself Don Quixote. Then he remembered that the great knights of olden times were not satisfied with a simple name. They added the name of their kingdom or country. So he, like a good knight, added to his own name that of his province and called himself Don Quixote de la Mancha.

Now that his armor was scrubbed, his horse was named, and he himself was furnished with a new name as well, he knew that he lacked only one thing—a lady he might help in times of danger and love in times of peace. "For," he said to himself, remembering what he had read in the books of knightly adventures, "if I should come upon some giant, as knights errant ordinarily do, and if I should knock him to the ground with one blow, or cut him in two, perhaps, or finally make him yield to me, it would be only right and proper that I should have some lady to whom I might present him."

Now, you may believe that the heart of the knight danced with joy when he found a woman he might call his lady. For, they say, in the next village lived a healthy, hearty country girl with whom he was sometimes in love, though she had never known it or taken notice of him whatsoever. Her name was Aldonza Lorenzo, but he determined that she, too, should be renamed and should carry a title that would show she was a princess and great lady. Thus he decided to call her Dulcinea, a name that was romantic and musical enough for the lady of so brave a knight.

All that he lacked now was a squire to attend to his wishes and to accompany him and Rocinante on his search for adventure. For this purpose, he chose a poor plowman he met along the way, one who had many children, and who called himself Sancho Panza.

Fiction

from *Don Quixote de la Mancha* by Miguel de Cervantes, continued

One day, while they were journeying along, Sancho Panza said to his master, "I pray you take good ear, Sir Knight, and that you remember that you have promised to make me the governor of an island, for I will know how to govern it no matter how great it may be."

And Don Quixote replied, "Thou must understand, friend Sancho, that it was a custom of ancient knights errant to make their squires governors of the islands and kingdoms they conquered, and I promise you that this excellent custom will be kept up by me. And if thou livest and I live, it may well be that I might conquer a kingdom and crown thee king of it."

Stop and Record

Make notes in the "Characters" section of the Fiction Organizer (page 131). Which characters are important to this part of the novel?

"By the same token," said Sancho Panza, "if I were a king, then should Joan, my wife, become a queen and my children princes?"

"There is no doubt of that," agreed Don Quixote.

"But I have doubt," replied Sancho. "For I think that even if it rained kingdoms down on earth, Joan would not be right for any of them. She would just not do as a queen. She might scrape by as a countess, but I have my doubts of that, too."

As they were talking, they caught sight of some thirty or forty windmills on a plain that lay ahead of them. When Don Quixote saw them, he said to his squire, "Behold, friend Sancho, in the distance there are thirty or forty monstrous giants with whom I mean to do battle. I will kill each of them and take their riches as reward for clearing away these evil fellows from the face of the earth."

"What giants?" asked Sancho, amazed.

"Those thou seest there," replied his master, "with the long arms."

"Take care, sir," cried Sancho, "for what we see there are not giants but windmills, and those things that appear to be their arms are the sails that are turned by the wind."

"It is clear," answered Don Quixote, "that thou art unused to adventures. They are giants, and if thou art afraid, get thee back home, and I will enter into fierce and unequal battle with them."

from *Don Quixote de la Mancha* by Miguel de Cervantes, continued

After saying this, he gave the spur to Rocinante, all the while ignoring Sancho Panza's cries that he was going to attack windmills and not giants. He shouted to the windmills in a loud voice, "Fly not, cowards and vile creatures, for it is only one knight that comes against you to do battle!"

At this moment, however, a slight breeze sprang up, and the great sail arms on the windmills began to move. Seeing this, Don Quixote shouted out again, "Although you have more arms than a Greek monster, you have to reckon with me!"

Saying this, he charged at Rocinante's best gallop and attacked the first mill in front of him. When he thrust his sword through the sail, the wind turned it with such violence that it broke his weapon into slivers, carrying him and his horse up and whirling around, till they finally tumbled off, rolling over the plain, the knight being terribly damaged.

Stop and Record
*Make notes in the "Plot" section of the Fiction Organizer (page 131).
What is Don Quixote doing, and why is he doing it?*

Sancho Panza hastened to help him, riding as fast as his long-eared donkey could go, and when he came up he found the knight unable to move, his shock at the fall being so great.

"Bless me," said Sancho, "did I not tell you that you should look carefully, for they were nothing more than windmills, and no one would ever think otherwise unless he had windmills for brains?"

"Peace, friend Sancho," said Don Quixote, "for the things of war are constantly changing, and I think this must be the work of one who has changed these giants into windmills to take from me the glory of the victory. But in the end, his wicked arts will do little good against my sword."

"May it prove so," said Sancho, as he helped his master rise and climb back onto Rocinante, who was also much bruised by the fall. And off again they rode, for there were other adventures waiting, other monsters to slay, other wrongs to make right.

Stop and Record
*Make notes in the "Style" section of the Fiction Organizer (page 131).
What is the tone of Cervantes's writing?*

Fiction

135

Using the Strategy

Use the strategy of synthesizing to help you zero in on one or more literary elements. For example, synthesizing can help you explore an author's style.

• Use the strategy of synthesizing to analyze a writer's style.

Style is the way writers use language to match their ideas. To understand a writer's style, look at these three elements: word choice, sentence structure, and literary devices.

Directions: Review the definition for *style* on page 403 of your handbook. Then answer these questions about Cervantes's style.

Style Chart

1. What unusual words did you notice in the excerpt?
2. What is Cervantes's language like? Is it formal or informal, modern or old-fashioned?
3. What are Cervantes's sentences like? Are they mostly long or short, simple or complex?
4. What literary devices—figurative language, symbols, and imagery—does Cervantes use?

Understanding How Novels Are Organized

Most plots progress in chronological, or time, order.

- **You can use Sequence Notes to keep track of the sequence of events the author describes.**

Directions: Write the events that follow the first one given below.

Sequence Notes

1. Don Quixote reads stories about the knights of old.

2.

3.

4.

5.

6.

Fiction

E **Connect**

Making connections to a novel can enhance your enjoyment of the reading.

• **Reacting to individual lines can help you connect to the plot, characters, and style of the work.**

Directions: Read the quotes from *Don Quixote de la Mancha* in the left column. Tell how they make you feel in the right column.

Double-entry Journal

Quotes	My thoughts and reactions
"So eagerly did the man plunge into the readings of these books that he often spent whole days and nights poring over them. . . ."	
"Thus he decided to call her Dulcinea, a name that was romantic and musical enough for the lady of so brave a knight."	
"He shouted to the windmills in a loud voice, 'Fly not, cowards and vile creatures, for it is only one knight that comes against you to do battle!' "	
"When he thrust his sword through the sail, the wind turned it with such violence that it broke his weapon into slivers, carrying him and his horse up and whirling around, till they finally tumbled off, rolling over the plain, the knight being terribly damaged."	
" 'Bless me,' said Sancho, 'did I not tell you that you should look carefully, for they were nothing more than windmills, and no one would ever think otherwise unless he had windmills for brains?' "	

After Reading

At this point, take a few minutes to process what you've learned. Once again, the strategy of synthesizing can help.

F Pause and Reflect

Think back on your reading and the major elements of the novel.

• **Ask yourself, "How well did I meet my purpose?"**

<u>Directions:</u> Put an X in the column that tells how well you understand the elements in this novel.

▸ **Checklist**

Element	I understand it very well.	I need to understand it better.
characters		
setting		
plot		

G Reread

When you reread, focus on one or more of the literary elements. Create a graphic organizer that can help you keep track of what you discover.

• **Use graphic organizers to process information from the novel.**

<u>Directions:</u> Reread the parts that tell about Don Quixote—what he looks like, acts like, says, and so on. Then fill in this Character Map.

▸ **Character Map**

What he says and does	What others think about him

Don Quixote

How he feels about others	How I feel about him

Fiction

Remember

Good readers make an effort to remember what they've read.

- **To help you remember a novel, give it a rating and then explain your choice.**

<u>**Directions:**</u> Rate the excerpt from *Don Quixote*. Then explain your opinion.

Rating Chart for a Novel

Plot
1   2   3   4   5   6   7   8   9   10
Dull   Interesting   Very interesting

Characters
1   2   3   4   5   6   7   8   9   10
Not believable   Somewhat believable   Very believable

Setting
1   2   3   4   5   6   7   8   9   10
Not developed   Somewhat developed   Well developed

Style
1   2   3   4   5   6   7   8   9   10
Not engaging   Somewhat engaging   Very engaging

Why I gave the ratings I did:

_____

_____

_____

_____

_____

Focus on **Characters**

Understanding a story's main character or characters can help you understand the plot, theme, and minor characters in the work. Follow these steps to analyze a main character.

Step 1: Make notes on what the character does and says.

Directions: Read the following paragraphs from a novel. Highlight information about one of the main characters, a man named Onion John.

from *Onion John* by Joseph Krumgold

Onion John was a lot different from anyone I ever hung out with before. Like his age. No one actually knew how old he'd be. But considering he was six feet and three inches tall with a mustache, it was a good guess that Onion John was well along in his years.

He used to live up on Hessian Hill, Onion John did, in a house he built out of piled up stone and four bathtubs and no running water. Once a month he'd get up in the middle of the night, according to the way the moon was, to cook up a stew with chunks of lead in it and maybe some chipped stone he collected and half a rabbit sometimes and always a little wood alcohol to make a blue flame. It wasn't a stew for eating. It was to get gold out of the moon, to make his fortune.

I never saw any fortune come out of what Onion John was cooking. And now I guess I never will. Because everything's changed for Onion John, on account of us getting to be friends the way we did.

It happened the day we played Rockton Township for the Little League Pennant. Onion John didn't come out to watch the ball game, actually. He came to go shopping in the garbage dump behind center field, which is the position that I play. The Serenity dump for John was the same as the supermarket is for most people. He went there for whatever he needed. And if he didn't find what he was looking for he usually came across something he could use just as well. So the sight of Onion John out there on the garbage dump, that day, there was nothing too different in that.

Fiction

Step 2: Create a Character Map.

Next, create a Character Map. Use it to keep track of your thoughts about the character.

Directions: Complete this Character Map on Onion John.

Character Map

How the character looks and feels

What others think about the character

Onion John

What the character does

How I feel about the character

NAME ....

Step 3: Make inferences about the character.

Finally, make some inferences, or reasonable guesses, about the character.

Directions: Describe the character's actions in Column 1. Write your inferences about Onion John in Column 2. The first one is done for you.

Inference Chart

What the Character Does	My Inferences About the Character
He lives in a house built of piled up stone and no running water.	He is not wealthy.

Fiction

Focus on Setting

*Setting is where and when the action takes place.
It affects the plot, the mood, and the characters
of a story. Follow these steps to analyze a setting.*

Step 1: Do a close reading.

Directions: Read this excerpt from the novel *M.C. Higgins, the Great.*
Highlight clues about time of day. Underline clues about place. Then
complete the Setting Chart for *M.C. Higgins, the Great.*

---

from *M.C. Higgins, the Great* by Virginia Hamilton

Mayo Cornelius Higgins raised his arms high to the sky and spread them wide.
He glanced furtively around. It was all right. There was no one to see his greeting
to the coming sunrise. But the motion of his arms caused a flutter of lettuce leaves he
had bound to his wrist with rubber bands. Like bracelets of green feathers, the leaves
commenced to wave.

M.C., as he was called, felt warm, moist air surround him. Humidity trapped
in the hills clung to the mountainside as the night passed on. In seconds, his skin grew
clammy. But he paid no attention to the oppressive heat with its odors of summer
growth and decay. For he was staring out over a grand sweep of hills, whose rolling
outlines grew clearer by the minute. As he stood on the gallery of his home, the
outcropping on which he lived on the mountainside seemed to fade out from under
him. I'm standing in midair, he thought.

Setting Chart

Clues about time	Clues about place
time of day:	where the story takes place:
season of the year:	

Step 2: Draw conclusions about the mood.

The setting can affect the mood, or atmosphere, of a story. For example, a beautiful setting can create a joyful mood. An ugly setting can create a gloomy mood.

Directions: Describe the setting and mood of *M.C. Higgins, the Great* here.

Inference Chart

What the scene looks like	My inference about the mood

Step 3: Draw conclusions about the characters.

Setting can also give you clues about characters. A character's response to the setting can tell you a lot about the character's personality.

Directions: In the left column, describe how the setting makes M.C. Higgins feel. Then write your inferences about him in the right column.

Inference Chart

The scene makes M.C. feel	My inference about him

Fiction

Focus on Dialogue

To focus on dialogue, pay attention to who is speaking, what is being said, and how it is being said. Follow these steps to analyze a piece of dialogue.

Step 1: Do a careful reading.

First, read the piece of dialogue slowly and carefully. Make notes as you go.

Directions: Read this excerpt from "The Adventure of the Dying Detective." Make notes.

from "The Adventure of the Dying Detective" by Sir Arthur Conan Doyle

"Well, Watson, we seem to have fallen upon evil days," said [Sherlock Holmes] in a feeble voice, but with something of his old carelessness of manner.

"My dear fellow!" I cried, approaching him.

"Stand back! Stand right back!" said he with the sharp imperiousness which I had associated only with moments of crisis. "If you approach me, Watson, I shall order you out of the house."

"But why?"

"Because it is my desire. Is that not enough?"

Yes, Mrs. Hudson was right. He was more masterful than ever. It was pitiful, however, to see his exhaustion.

"I only wished to help," I explained.

"Exactly! You will help best by doing what you are told."

"Certainly, Holmes."

He relaxed the austerity of his manner. "You are not angry?" he asked, gasping for breath.

Poor devil, how could I be angry when I saw him lying in such a plight before me?

..
and ....
are talking.

They sound ....

They are talking about ....

NAME ....

Step 2: Look for clues about character.

Next, look for what the dialogue reveals about each character.

Directions: Write something each character says. Then write what you can infer about the character from the words.

Inference Chart

What character says	My inferences about the character
Watson:	
Holmes:	

Step 3: Look for clues about plot.

Then, think about the story's plot. Dialogue often can give you clues about what's going to happen next.

Directions: Predict what you think will happen next in "The Adventure of the Dying Detective." Then explain your prediction.

My prediction: ....

Why I think this will happen: ....

....

Step 4: Look for clues about mood.

What the characters say and how they say it can affect a story's mood.

Directions: Tell the mood of this scene from "The Adventure of the Dying Detective."

Mood: ....

Words of a character that help to create the mood: ....

Fiction

147

NAME ....

FOR USE WITH PAGES 368–375

Focus on Plot

Plot is the series of interrelated events that connects the beginning of a story to the end.

Step 1: Track the key events.

In a well-written plot, one event leads into another, very much like stairs on a staircase.

Directions: The events below are from "Little Red Cap," sometimes called "Little Red Riding Hood," by the Brothers Grimm. Number them in the correct order and draw sketches to reflect the action.

_____The wolf goes directly to the grandmother's house, where he swallows her whole.

_____Little Red Cap arrives and says, "Grandmother, what big ears you have!"

_____Little Red Cap vows, "As long as I live, I will never leave the path to run into the woods, when my mother has forbidden me to do so."

_____Little Red Cap sets out, meets the wolf, and wanders off to pick flowers.

_____The huntsman rescues Little Red Cap and her grandmother from the wolf's stomach.

_____The wolf eats Little Red Cap.

1.	2.	3.
4.	5.	6.

Step 2: Analyze the conflict.

Next, think about central conflict in the work.

Directions: Read some lines from "Little Red Cap." Then explain the story's central conflict.

> ### from "Little Red Cap" by the Brothers Grimm
>
> "Good day, Little Red Cap," said the wolf.
>
> "Thank you kindly, wolf," answered she.
>
> "Where are you going, Little Red Cap?" asked the wolf.
>
> "To my grandmother's."
>
> "What have you got in your apron?"
>
> "Cakes. Yesterday was baking day, so poor sick Grandmother is to have something good, to make her stronger."
>
> "Where does your grandmother live, Little Red Cap?"
>
> "A quarter of an hour farther on in the wood. Her house stands under the three large oak trees. You surely must know it," said Little Red Cap.
>
> The wolf thought to himself, "What a tender young creature! What a nice plump mouthful—she will be better to eat than the old woman. I must act craftily, so as to catch both."

The conflict is ....

....

....

Step 3: Think about plot and theme.

Sometimes the events of a plot can help you understand the writer's message, or theme.

Directions: Look back at the events listed in Step 1 and the lines from the story in Step 2. What do you think the message in the story is? Write a journal entry about the theme.

Journal Response

Theme of "Little Red Cap": ....

....

....

Focus on  Theme

Theme is the writer's message, or main idea. Usually a writer will scatter clues about theme throughout a work. Your job is to find the clues and put them together.

Step 1: Find the "big ideas" or general topics.

Sometimes the title of the piece will give you a clue about the author's big ideas.

Directions: Read these titles. Write what you think are the big ideas. One has been done for you.

<u>Brave New World</u> bravery	<u>Absolutely Normal Chaos</u>
<u>The Song of Hiawatha</u>	<u>Journey to Topaz</u>

Step 2: Look for what characters do or say.

Next, find details in the text that relate to the big ideas you've identified. Begin by thinking about what the characters say and do.

Directions: Read these quotes from *Don Quixote de la Mancha* by Miguel de Cervantes. Tell how they relate to Cervantes's big idea of "bravery."

Double-entry Journal

Quote	What I think about it
"He was certain that these books presented accurate histories of events that occurred in the days of chivalry."	
"'What giants?' asked Sancho, amazed."	

Step 3: Decide on the author's point, or message, about the big idea.

Remember that theme is the point the author wants to make about the topic.

Directions: Think about what you've read from *Don Quixote de la Mancha*. What do you think Cervantes wants to say about bravery?

His message about bravery: ....

....

....

Step 4: Put it all together.

Once you've identified a theme, decide which examples and details from the text support it.

Directions: Complete this organizer. Use your notes from *Don Quixote de la Mancha* (pages 129–140).

Fiction

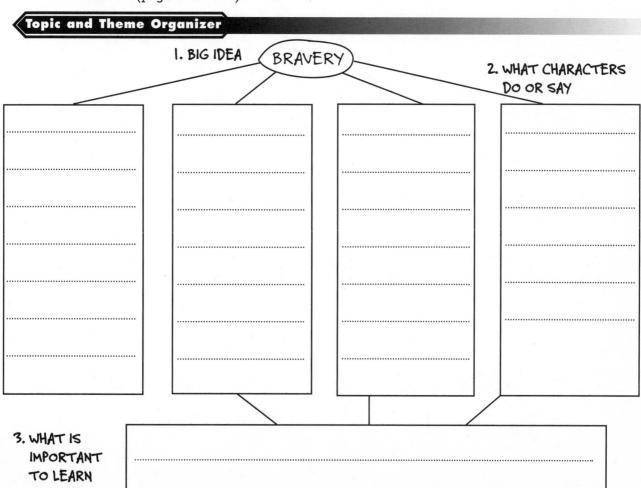

Topic and Theme Organizer

1. BIG IDEA BRAVERY 2. WHAT CHARACTERS DO OR SAY

3. WHAT IS IMPORTANT TO LEARN

Focus on Comparing and Contrasting

You can compare and contrast a single element in two works—for example, setting to setting, or character to character. Follow these steps to make a comparison.

Step 1: Read.

As a first step, read both works carefully. Think about the element and how it is similar and different in the two works.

Directions: Read these two novel excerpts. Make notes about the characters described.

from *Crash* by Jerry Spinelli

My real name is John. John Coogan. But everybody calls me Crash, even my parents.

It started way back when I got my first football helmet for Christmas. I don't really remember this happening, but they say that when my uncle Herm's family came over to see our presents, as they were coming through the front door I got down into a four-point stance, growled, "Hut! Hut! Hut!" and charged ahead with my brand-new helmet. Seems I knocked my cousin Bridget clear back out the doorway. . . .

Like I said, personally I don't remember the whole thing, but looking back at what I do remember about myself, I'd have to say the story is probably true. As far as I can tell, I've always been crashing—into people, into things, you name it, with or without a helmet.

from *The Root Cellar* by Janet Lunn

Every afternoon she was free to do as she pleased. Wet days she read or explored the hotel. Fine days she poked around shops or went to museums or movies in foreign languages. She often sat for hours in parks, watching people— old people feeding the birds, shoppers, strollers, mothers or fathers with their children. Rose had never known other children and they fascinated her. She often longed to speak to them, sometimes even to become a part of their games, but they frightened her. They were apt to be rough and make loud jokes, and she was afraid she wouldn't know what to say to them.

What I know about John:

....

....

What I know about Rose:

....

....

NAME ....

Step 2: Organize.

Next, organize what you know about the element to be compared.

Directions: Complete this Venn Diagram.

Venn Diagram

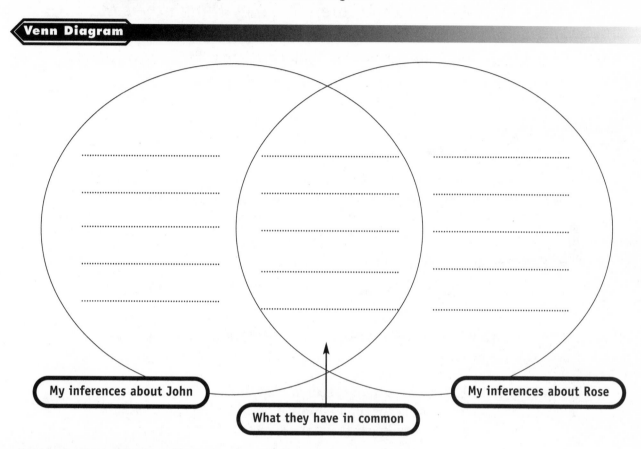

My inferences about John

What they have in common

My inferences about Rose

Step 3: Draw conclusions.

Draw conclusions about the similarities and differences between the two elements.

Directions: Answer these questions about the two characters.

How are the two characters similar? ....

....

How are they different? ....

....

....

....

Fiction

Reading a Poem

Poets choose their words carefully. They think about the look, sound, and meaning of each word. Good readers know that reading poetry involves looking for meaning, listening for sounds, and visualizing images.

Before Reading

Reading poetry takes practice. Use the reading process and the strategy of close reading to help you get more from every poem you read. Try it here, with stanzas from the classic poem *The Song of Hiawatha*.

A Set a Purpose

Your purpose for reading a poem is twofold. First, find out what the poem is about. Second, figure out what it means.

• **To set your purpose, ask a question about the subject and meaning of the poem.**

Directions: Write your purpose for reading Longfellow's "Hiawatha's Childhood," a section from the long narrative poem *The Song of Hiawatha*. Then tell what you already know about the subject.

My purpose: ....

....

....

....

What I already know about Hiawatha or the poem: ....

....

....

....

....

B Preview

As a first step, preview the poem you are about to read. Look at the title and name of the poet. Read any introduction or background. Check for rhyme and repeated words. Then read the first and last lines carefully.

Directions: Preview "Hiawatha's Childhood." Make notes below.

Preview Notes

The title:

The poet's name:

I learned this from the background information:

I saw these repeated words and names:

In the first line, I noticed this:

In the last line, I noticed this:

Here's what I noticed about the shape and structure of the poem:

Poetry

"Hiawatha's Childhood" by Henry Wadsworth Longfellow

About the Poem and the Poet

Hiawatha was a legendary Native American chief. He is thought to have been responsible for helping to form the Iroquois League in which five powerful Iroquois nations—the Senecas, Onondagas, Mohawks, Cayugas, and Oneidas—joined forces to bring about the "Great Peace." According to legend, Hiawatha's mother died shortly after his birth, and he was raised by his grandmother, Nokomis.

Henry Wadsworth Longfellow was one of the most admired poets of his time, recognized for his narrative poems about America's past. In "Hiawatha's Childhood" from The Song of Hiawatha, *he celebrates Hiawatha's life and achievements.*

By the shores of Gitchie Gumee,
By the shining Big-Sea-Water,
Stood the wigwam of Nokomis,
Daughter of the Moon, Nokomis.
Dark behind it rose the forest,
Rose the black and gloomy pine trees,
Rose the firs with cones upon them;
Bright before it beat the water,
Beat the clear and sunny water,
Beat the shining Big-Sea-Water.

There the wrinkled old Nokomis
Nursed the little Hiawatha,
Rocked him in his linden cradle,
Bedded soft in moss and rushes,
Safely bound with reindeer sinews;
Stilled his fretful wail by saying,
"Hush! the Naked Bear will hear thee!"
Lulled him into slumber, singing,
"Ewa-yea! my little owlet!
Who is this, that lights the wigwam?
With his great eyes lights the wigwam?
Ewa-yea! my little owlet!"

"Hiawatha's Childhood" by Henry Wadsworth Longfellow, continued

Many things Nokomis taught him
Of the stars that shine in heaven;
Showed him Ishkoodah, the comet,
Ishkoodah, with fiery tresses;
Showed the Death Dance of the spirits,
Warriors with their plumes and war clubs,
Flaring far away to northward
In the frosty nights of winter;
Showed the broad white road in heaven,
Pathway of the ghosts, the shadows,
Running straight across the heavens,
Crowded with the ghosts, the shadows.

At the door on summer evenings,
Sat the little Hiawatha;
Heard the whispering of the pine trees,
Heard the lapping of the waters,
Sounds of music, words of wonder;
"Minne-wawa!" said the pine trees,
"Mudway-aushka!" said the water.

Saw the firefly, Wah-wah-taysee,
Flitting through the dusk of evening,
With the twinkle of its candle
Lighting up the brakes and bushes,
And he sang the song of children,
Sang the song Nokomis taught him:
"Wah-wah-taysee, little firefly,
Little, flitting, white-fire insect,
Little, dancing, white-fire creature,
Light me with your little candle,
Ere upon my bed I lay me,
Ere in sleep I close my eyelids!"

Poetry

"Hiawatha's Childhood" by Henry Wadsworth Longfellow, continued

Saw the moon rise from the water,
Rippling, rounding from the water,
Saw the flecks and shadows on it,
Whispered, "What is that, Nokomis?"
And the good Nokomis answered:
"Once a warrior, very angry,
Seized his grandmother, and threw her
Up into the sky at midnight;
Right against the moon he threw her;
Tis her body that you see there."

Saw the rainbow in the heaven,
In the eastern sky, the rainbow,
Whispered, "What is that, Nokomis?"
And the good Nokomis answered:
"'Tis the heaven of flowers you see there;
All the wild flowers of the forest,
All the lilies of the prairie,
When on earth they fade and perish,
Blossom in that heaven above us."

When he heard the owls at midnight,
Hooting, laughing in the forest,
"What is that?" he cried in terror,
"What is that," he said, "Nokomis?"
And the good Nokomis answered:
"That is but the owl and owlet,
Talking in their native language,
Talking, scolding at each other."

Then the little Hiawatha
Learned of every bird its language,
Learned their names and all their secrets,
How they built their nests in summer,
Where they hid themselves in winter,
Talked with them whene'er he met them,
Called them "Hiawatha's Chickens."

NAME ....

"Hiawatha's Childhood" by Henry Wadsworth Longfellow, continued

Of all beasts he learned the language,
Learned their names and all their secrets,
How the beavers built their lodges,
Where the squirrels hid their acorns,
How the reindeer ran so swiftly,
Why the rabbit was so timid,
Talked with them whene'er he met them,
Called them "Hiawatha's Brothers."

C Plan

A good strategy for poetry is close reading.
Careful reading of poetry usually
means reading a poem
at least three times.

- **Use the strategy of close reading with poetry.**

Even if you read through a poem several times, you will still need a reading strategy. Probably the best strategy for reading poems is called **close reading.** That means going word by word, line by line poem. It works best with short poems. The plan for reading and rereading a poem four times is, in a way, a kind of close reading.

A reading tool called a Double-entry Journal is a good way of doing close reading and responding to a text. Part of text appears on the left side the lines or your atten or important the right, t to the wo how yo about the ieve.

Poetry

During Reading

 D ## Read with a Purpose

On your first reading, read for enjoyment. On your second reading, read for meaning. On your third reading, read for structure and feeling.

Directions: Read Longfellow's poem three times. After each reading, make some notes on this chart.

Plan for Reading a Poem

First Reading	Second Reading	Third Reading
Here's **what I liked** about the poem:	I think Longfellow's **message** is this:	Here's what I noticed about the **structure and feeling** . . . rhythm: images: mood:

Close reading means reading word for word, line for line. To use the strategy, create a Double-entry Journal. It can help you respond to individual lines of the poem.

• **Use a Double-entry Journal to organize your thoughts and feelings about a poem.**

Directions: Read the lines from Longfellow's poem in the left column. Write what you think the words mean or how they make you feel in the right column.

Double-entry Journal

Quote	My Thoughts
"Dark behind it rose the forest, Rose the black and gloomy pine trees,"	
"Then the little Hiawatha Learned of every bird its language, Learned their names and all their secrets,"	

Understanding How Poems Are Organized

Knowing how a poem is organized can help you find what you're looking for when you're reading.

Directions: Do a close reading of this stanza. Then complete the sticky notes. If you need help with poetry terms, see pages 446–469 in your handbook.

I noticed these repeated words:

Saw the moon rise from the water,
Rippling, rounding from the water,
Saw the flecks and shadows on it,
Whispered, "What is that, Nokomis?"
And the good Nokomis answered:
"Once a warrior, very angry,
Seized his grandmother, and threw her
Up into the sky at midnight;
Right against the moon he threw her;
'Tis her body that you see there."

The image I see is

Poetry

Connect

Making a personal connection to a word, line, or stanza can strengthen your understanding of the poem's meaning.

• Record how the poem makes you feel.

Directions: Reread the final page of "Hiawatha's Childhood." Then tell how Longfellow's words make you feel.

This is what I feel about Nokomis:

....

....

This is what I feel about Hiawatha:

....

....

This is what I feel about the whole poem:

....

....

My favorite part is this: because

....

....

After Reading

After your third reading, take the time to think about what you know.

Pause and Reflect

At this point, you'll want to return to your reading purpose. When you finish a poem, ask yourself, "How well did I meet my purpose?"

Directions: Circle *have* or *have not* below and explain your choice.

I feel I have / have not met my reading purpose. Here's why:

....

....

....

....

G Reread

Use the rereading strategy of paraphrasing to focus on particular lines in the poem—perhaps the ones you liked best or the ones you didn't understand.

• **A powerful rereading strategy to use with poetry is paraphrasing.**

Directions: Read the lines in the first column. Write a paraphrase of the lines in the second column.

Paraphrase Chart

Lines	My Paraphrase
"There the wrinkled old Nokomis Nursed the little Hiawatha, Rocked him in his linden cradle,"	
"And he sang the song of children, Sang the song Nokomis taught him: 'Wah-wah-taysee, little firefly,' "	

H Remember

Good readers remember what they "saw" while reading a poem.

• **Making a sketch can help you remember a poem's subject.**

Directions: Make a sketch of "Hiawatha's Childhood."

Journal Sketch

Caption:

Poetry

Focus on Language

One part of the richness of poetry is its language. Poets know how to make every word count. Follow these steps to analyze the language of a poem.

Step 1: Read and take notes.

First, read the poem the whole way through without stopping. Then read it a second time. Highlight words that suggest unusual ideas, striking imagery, and strong emotions.

Directions: Read these stanzas from "Jabberwocky," a famous poem by Lewis Carroll. Use a highlighter to mark two words in each line that catch your attention.

from "Jabberwocky" by Lewis Carroll

'Twas brillig, and the slithy toves
    Did gyre and gimble in the wabe;
All mimsy were the borogoves,
    And the mome raths outgrabe.

"Beware the Jabberwock, my son!
    The jaws that bite, the claws that catch!
Beware the Jubjub bird, and shun
    The frumious Bandersnatch!"

He took his vorpal sword in hand:
    Long time the manxome foe he sought—
So rested he by the Tumtum tree,
    And stood awhile in thought.

And, as in uffish thought he stood,
    The Jabberwock, with eyes of flame,
Came whiffling through the tulgey wood,
    And burbled as it came!

Step 2: Find key words.

As a second step, read the poem again. Many of the words in "Jabberwocky" are made-up words, but others are words you recognize. It's important to understand the meaning of these words.

Directions: Reread "Jabberwocky." Write a short definition for each word below. If necessary, use a dictionary.

beware: ....

sword: ....

shun: ....

flame: ....

Step 3: Look for imagery.

Finish by looking for imagery in the poem. What pictures created by the words appeal to your senses of sight, hearing, smell, touch, or taste?

Directions: Look at these examples of imagery in "Jabberwocky." Tell what you think the phrases mean and what sense or senses you use to experience the words. Then find your own example of imagery.

Imagery Chart

Imagery from the poem	What I think it means	What sense I use
"The jaws that bite, the claws that catch!"		
"The Jabberwock, with eyes of flame,"		

Focus on Meaning

Use the reading process and the strategy of close reading to help you understand the meaning of a poem. Follow these steps.

Step 1: Think about the poem's language.

First, read the poem the whole way through without stopping. Try to get an idea of what it is about. Then read the poem again. Make notes about important or interesting words.

Directions: Read "Remember." Complete the sticky notes.

"Remember" by Christina Rossetti

Christina Rossetti (1830–1894) is one of the most important of the English poets. She specialized in works of fantasy, poems for children, and religious works. Because she was ill for much of her life, Rossetti's poems often convey a sense of sadness or yearning.

Remember me when I am gone away,
    Gone far away into the silent land,
    When you can no more hold me by the hand,
Nor I half turn to go yet turning stay.
Remember me when no more day by day
    You tell me of our future that you planned:
    Only remember me; you understand
It will be late to counsel then or pray.
Yet if you should forget me for a while
    And afterwards remember, do not grieve:
    For if the darkness and corruption leave
    A vestige of the thoughts that once I had,
Better by far that you should forget and smile
    Than that you should remember and be sad.

The background section tells me
_____
_____
_____

The word remember makes me feel
_____
_____
_____
_____

Grieve is
_____
kind of word.
_____

Step 2: Consider what's unusual and important.

Next, reread the poem line by line. Look for unusual and important words or ideas. Mark the two words or ideas in each line that seem important to you.

Directions: Write two important words from each line in the poem.
Then write your ideas about the meaning.

Two Per Line

Words	My Ideas

Poetry

Step 3: Explore your feelings.

Next, note your personal response to the poem. This can help you explore the meaning of the poem.

Directions: Answer these questions. Refer to your notes as needed.

What did you picture as you were reading the poem? ....

How do the speaker's words make you feel? ....

....

Step 4: Decide what the poet is saying.

Finish by figuring out what the poet is trying to say. What message does he or she have for readers? This formula can help.

topic of the poem + what the poet is saying about the topic = poem's message

topic of "Remember"	What Rossetti says	poem's message
.... +	.... =	....
....	....	....
....	....	....
....	....	....

Directions: Paraphrase, or retell, lines from "Remember." Write your notes on the Paraphrase Chart.

Paraphase Chart

Quote	My Paraphrase
"Remember me when no more day by day You tell me of our future that you planned. . ."	

Focus on Sound and Structure

Examining the sound and structure can increase your enjoyment and understanding of a poem. Follow these steps.

Step 1: Examine the organization.

Begin by reading the poem the whole way through without stopping. Then take a moment to examine how the poem looks on the page.

Directions: Read the poem "Break, Break, Break." Make notes.

"Break, Break, Break" by Alfred, Lord Tennyson

Break, break, break,
     On thy cold gray stones, O Sea!
And I would that my tongue could utter
     The thoughts that arise in me.

O, well for the fisherman's boy,
     That he shouts with his sister at play!
O, well for the sailor lad,
     That he sings in his boat on the bay.

And the stately ships go on
     To their haven under the hill;
But O for the touch of a vanish'd hand,
     And the sound of a voice that is still!

Break, break, break,
     At the foot of the crags, O Sea!
But the tender grace of a day that is dead
     Will never come back to me.

The poem has _____ lines.

I noticed this about the words:

I noticed this about the punctuation:

Poetry

169

Step 2: Look for repeated words and sounds.

Next, listen to the "music" of the poem. What do the words *sound* like?

Directions: Reread the poem. Highlight repeated words. Circle repeated sounds. Write what you noticed in this chart.

Repeated Words	Repeated Sounds
break	

Step 3: Listen to the rhyme.

Rhyme contributes to the overall effect of the poem. You can use letters to show the rhyme pattern. For example:

> Break, break, break   a
>   On thy cold gray stones, O Sea!   b
> And I would that my tongue could utter   c
>   The thoughts that arise in me.   b

Directions: Return to the poem. Use letters to show the rhyme scheme. Write the letters next to each line.

Step 4: Listen for rhythm.

Review the definition of rhythm on page 463 of your handbook. Can you hear a regular rhythm or "beat" in "Break, Break, Break"?

Directions: Whisper Tennyson's poem to yourself. Then tell about the pattern of beats in these lines from the poem. (Hint: How does the poem sound like the movement of waves?)

"And I would that my tongue could utter,
....

The thoughts that arise in me."
....

Reading a  Play

The action of a play is told through dialogue and stage directions. When you read a play, stay alert and "listen" to what the characters are saying. Try to visualize what the characters are "seeing."

Before Reading

Practice reading a play here. Use the reading process and the strategy of summarizing to help you get more from the classic drama *Pyramus and Thisbe.*

 A ### Set a Purpose

Your purpose for reading a play is to find out about the three major literary elements of drama.

• **To set your purpose, ask questions about the characters, conflict, and theme of the play.**

Directions: Write three purpose-setting questions for reading *Pyramus and Thisbe* here. Then tell what you already know about this story.

My purpose: ....

....

....

....

What I know: ....

....

....

....

Drama

B **Preview**

When you preview a play, pay attention to any introductory material, including the title page and cast of characters.

• Previewing a play helps you know what to expect during your careful reading.

<u>Directions:</u> Preview the title page and the first several lines of *Pyramus and Thisbe* (pages 173–175). Complete the sticky notes.

Pyramus and Thisbe

A Play Based on the Fable by Thomas Bulfinch

CAST OF CHARACTERS

Pyramus, a young Babylonian man

Thisbe, a young Babylonian woman

SETTING

TIME: one summer evening and the next day

PLACE: ancient Babylonia

The title of the play is:

These are the two main characters:

Here's what I noticed after skimming the first several lines:

This comes to mind when I read the information about the setting:

NAME

Based on *Pyramus and Thisbe*

Act I, Scene 1

PYRAMUS *is the handsomest youth, and* THISBE *the fairest maiden, in all of Babylonia. Their parents occupy adjoining houses, and so the young people get to know each other. Their acquaintance eventually ripens into love. They would gladly have married, but their parents forbade it. Even so, the love between* PYRAMUS *and* THISBE *grows more intense, as forbidden love is wont to do. One day, with their hearts close to breaking for having not seen each other,* PYRAMUS *and* THISBE *discover a crack in the wall that separates the two houses.*

PYRAMUS *(With great sadness).* Cruel wall! Why must you keep two lovers apart?

THISBE *(Gently).* Pyramus, complain no more about the wall, nor call it cruel. We owe this wall the privilege of transmitting loving words to willing ears.

PYRAMUS *(Kissing the crack that allows the two lovers to hear one another).* Beloved Thisbe, your words are true. But the wall between us, though it is our ally, is more than I can bear. Tomorrow, Thisbe, let us slip away from watchful eyes and walk the fields.

Stop and Record

Scene 1: Fill in the "characters" and "setting" boxes of your Fiction Organizer (page 176).

THISBE *(Excitedly).* Is it possible, Pyramus?

PYRAMUS. Trust in me, my sweet. Meet me in the garden by the monument of Ninus. If you should arrive first, wait at the foot of the white mulberry tree. If I arrive first, I shall do the same. Until then my fair Thisbe—

*(*PYRAMUS *and* THISBE *kiss the wall that separates them and rush hurriedly off the stage.)*

Stop and Record

Scene 1: Fill in the "plot" box of your Fiction Organizer (page 176).

Based on *Pyramus and Thisbe*, continued

Act I, Scene 2

The next evening. THISBE, *her hair covered in a long veil, waits at the foot of the white mulberry tree for her lover to arrive. Nearby is a small spring.* THISBE *reaches for a taste of the cool water and catches sight of a lioness on the opposite side of the spring. The lioness, her mouth bloody from a recent kill, stoops to take a drink of water.*

THISBE *(Fearfully).* Bold lioness, queen of the jungle! I fear you, though you cannot see me in the gloom. But hide I must, and wait for brave Pyramus to arrive.

(THISBE *flees the stream and hides in the hollow of a rock across the field. In her haste, she drops her veil, which the lioness picks up in her bloody mouth. The lioness tears at the veil but drops it suddenly at the sound of approaching footsteps.*)

Stop and Record
Scene 2: Fill in the "characters" and "setting" boxes of your Fiction Organizer (page 176).

PYRAMUS *(Breathing hard, as if from running).* Thisbe! Where are you, fair maiden— But ho! What is this?

(PYRAMUS *looks down and sees the lioness's prints in the sand. He then spies the veil, which he picks up and clutches to his heart.*)

PYRAMUS *(Anguished).* O hapless girl! I have been the cause of your death! Thou, more worthy of life than I, has fallen the first victim. I will follow. I am the guilty cause, in tempting you forth to a place of such peril, and not being myself on the spot to guard you. Come forth from the rocks, ye lions, and tear at this guilty body with your teeth!

(PYRAMUS *turns toward the white mulberry tree, the veil still in his hand.*)

PYRAMUS *(With resolve).* My blood shall also stain your bark, for without my beloved Thisbe—

Based on *Pyramus and Thisbe*, continued

(PYRAMUS *plunges a sword into his heart. He falls to the ground, his wound spilling blood on the roots and trunk of the mulberry tree. At this moment,* THISBE *creeps out from her hiding spot and walks back toward the tree. She shudders when she sees the form of one struggling in the agonies of death and then breaks into a run toward the tree.*)

THISBE (*Recognizing her lover*). O Pyramus! What has done this? Answer me, Pyramus; it is your own Thisbe that speaks. Hear me dearest, and lift that drooping head.

(THISBE *sinks to the ground beside* PYRAMUS.)

THISBE (*Upon seeing the sword*). Why, your own hand has slain you, and for my sake. I too can be brave for once, and my love is as strong as yours. I will follow you in death, for I have been the cause; and death which alone could part us shall not prevent my joining you. And you, unhappy parents of us both, deny us not our united request. As love and death have joined us, let one tomb contain us. And thou, tree, retain the marks of the slaughter. Let your berries serve as memorials of our blood.

(So saying, THISBE *plunges the sword into her own heart.*)

The parents grant her wish, the two bodies are buried in one tomb, and the tree ever after brings forth purple berries, as it does to this day.

The End

Stop and Record
Scene 2: Fill in the "plot" box of your Fiction Organizer (page 176).

Drama

NAME ....

FOR USE WITH PAGES 472–488

C Plan

Next make a plan. You need a strategy that can help you find out about the characters, plot, and theme of the play.

• **Use the strategy of summarizing to help you meet your purpose for reading.**

During Reading

Now go back and do a careful reading of *Pyramus and Thisbe*.

D Read with a Purpose

Be sure to keep your reading purpose in mind as you read. Remember that you are searching for information about characters, conflict, and theme.

<u>Directions:</u> Record your notes on the Fiction Organizer below. They can help you keep track of the most important elements of the play.

Fiction Organizer

Characters		Characters

Scene 1		Scene 2

Setting	Plot	Setting	Plot

Write the setting of the scene here.

Summarize what happens in the scene here.

Write the setting of the scene here.

Summarize what happens in the scene here.

Using the Strategy

When you summarize a play, you tell the events of the plot in your own words. A Magnet Summary can help you organize information around key concepts called "magnet words." For example, one magnet word you might use for *Pyramus and Thisbe* is *love*.

• **Summarizing can help you process and remember what you've read.**

Directions: Write other words about the scenes you've just read. Then use all of the words, plus the "magnet word," to create a summary.

Magnet Summary

	Magnet Word	
	Love	

Summary

Drama

177

Understanding How
Plays Are Organized

The plots of plays usually have five parts: the exposition, the rising action, the climax, the falling action, and the resolution. A simple Plot Diagram can help you see the organization of the play.

• **To fully understand a play, examine the plot.**

Directions: Make notes about the five parts in *Pyramus and Thisbe*.

Plot Diagram

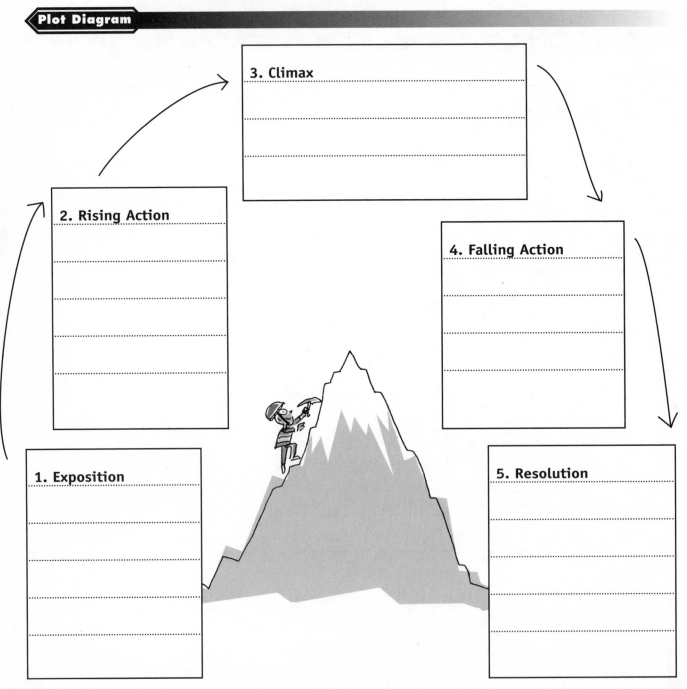

3. Climax

2. Rising Action

4. Falling Action

1. Exposition

5. Resolution

NAME ....

 E **Connect**

Making a personal connection to a play can help you understand the playwright's theme, or message. One way of connecting is to tell your opinions of the characters.

- **Responding to the characters can help you uncover the theme of a play.**

Directions: Tell how you feel about Pyramus and Thisbe. Then explain your opinion.

Here's how I feel about Pyramus:

....

....

Here's how I feel about Thisbe:

....

....

After Reading

When you finish reading, take a moment to think about the play's big ideas.

F **Pause and Reflect**

After reading, ask yourself about the characters, conflict, and theme.

- **After you finish a selection, go back to your original purpose and look for answers to your questions.**

Directions: How well did you meet your reading purpose? Make notes about any part of the scene that confuses or puzzles you.

....

....

....

....

Drama

Reread

At this point, you may need to think some more about the theme of the play. The rereading strategy of visualizing can help.

• **Visualizing can help you "see" a play's theme.**

Directions: Draw the scene under the white mulberry tree. Then write the playwright's lesson about love.

I think that this is the play's lesson about love:
....
....

 Remember

Good readers remember what they've read.

• **To remember a play, memorize and then react to key passages.**

Directions: Choose a short passage from *Pyramus and Thisbe* to memorize. Write the passage on the lines below. Then try to memorize this passage.

Passage from *Pyramus and Thisbe:* ....

....

....

....

....

Focus on Theme

Most plays have one central theme and one or more minor themes. Follow these steps to find a play's themes.

Step 1: Find the "big ideas" or general topics.

Begin by asking yourself, "What are some of the play's general topics?" Remember that some general topics appear over and over in literature. To jog your memory, these are just a few of them: courage, death, faith, hope, love, loyalty, trust, unhappiness, and war.

Directions: Get together with a partner. Make a list of two or three general topics in *Pyramus and Thisbe*. Write them here.

General Topics in *Pyramus and Thisbe*
Topic #1:
Topic #2:
Topic #3:

Drama

Step 2: Note what the characters do or say that relates to the general topics.

Next, think about the characters' reactions to the general topics.

Directions: With a partner, choose one general topic to discuss. Tell what Pyramus and Thisbe do and say that relates to the topic. Make notes here.

General Topic	
What Pyramus does or says:	What Thisbe does or says:

Step 3: Write a statement of the author's point or message about the general topics.

Be careful not to confuse a play's topic with its theme. The **topic** is what the play is about. The **theme** is the playwright's *message* about the topic. Use this formula to find a theme in *Pyramus and Thisbe*.

Write a general topic here.

Write the playwright's message about the topic here.

Write a theme statement here.

_____ + _____ = _____

_____ _____

Directions: Write a short opinion statement about one of the themes in *Pyramus and Thisbe*. Explain how it makes you feel.

Theme in *Pyramus and Thisbe*:
How I feel about it:

Focus on  Language

"Listening" to a playwright's language can help you find some important clues about characters, plot, and theme. Follow these steps to analyze the language of a play.

Step 1: Pay attention to key lines and speeches.

A character's speeches can help you understand his or her personality.

Directions: Read these speeches from *Pyramus and Thisbe*. Then write two adjectives (descriptive words) that describe Pyramus and two adjectives that describe Thisbe.

> **Based on *Pyramus and Thisbe***
>
> PYRAMUS *(Anguished)*. O hapless girl! I have been the cause of your death! Thou, more worthy of life than I, has fallen the first victim. I will follow. I am the guilty cause, in tempting you forth to a place of such peril, and not being myself on the spot to guard you. Come forth from the rocks, ye lions, and tear at this guilty body with your teeth!

Pyramus is _____ and _____.

> **Based on *Pyramus and Thisbe***
>
> THISBE *(Upon seeing the sword)*. Why, your own hand has slain you, and for my sake. I too can be brave for once, and my love is as strong as yours. I will follow you in death, for I have been the cause; and death which alone could part us shall not prevent my joining you. And you, unhappy parents of us both, deny us not our united request. As love and death have joined us, let one tomb contain us. And thou, tree, retain the marks of the slaughter. Let your berries serve as memorials of our blood.

Thisbe is _____ and _____.

Drama

Step 2: Read the stage directions.

Stage directions can help you "see" the events of a play.

Directions: Read these stage directions. Then sketch the scene's action on the Storyboard.

Based on *Pyramus and Thisbe*

(PYRAMUS *looks down and sees the lioness's prints in the sand. He then spies the veil, which he picks up and clutches to his heart.*)

Storyboard

1.	2.	3.

NAME ....

Step 3: Analyze the dialogue.

Dialogue can help you figure out a play's theme.

Directions: Find lines in this conversation that support the playwright's theme about the power of love. Write them in the organizer.

> **Based on *Pyramus and Thisbe***
>
> PYRAMUS *(With great sadness)*. Cruel wall! Why must you keep two lovers apart?
>
> THISBE *(Gently)*. Pyramus, complain no more about the wall, nor call it cruel. We owe this wall the privilege of transmitting loving words to willing ears.
>
> PYRAMUS *(Kissing the crack that allows the two lovers to hear one another)*. Beloved Thisbe, your words are true. But the wall between us, though it is our ally, is more than I can bear. . . .

Double-entry Journal

Quote	My Thoughts

Drama

Reading a Website

When you read a website, you jump around so much it's easy to get lost. Remember, too, that not all websites give reliable information. Your job as a critical reader is to zero in on the information you need and decide whether that information is reliable.

Before Reading

Practice using the reading process and the strategy of reading critically to help you "navigate" a website about asthma.

A Set a Purpose

It's easy to get distracted when reading a website. To prevent this problem, decide on a purpose *before* you visit the site.

• **To set your purpose, make a list of questions about the subject.**

Directions: Use this K-W-L Chart to list what you already know and what you want to find out about asthma. You will fill in what you learned later.

K-W-L Chart

What I **K**now	What I **W**ant to Know	What I **L**earned
	1. What are the symptoms of asthma?	

NAME

 Preview

As soon as you arrive at the website you're looking for, take a moment to survey it. Get a sense of what's offered before you begin clicking.

Directions: Preview the "Asthma and You" website. Look for the items on this checklist. Make notes on what you find.

Preview Checklist

✓ The name and overall look of the site

✓ The main menu or table of contents

✓ The first few lines describing the site

✓ Images or graphics that create a feeling for the site

✓ The source or sponsor of the site

Internet

http://www.iaa.asthma.com*

NEWS: The 3rd Annual Meeting of the International Asthma Association will be held November 2–5 at the Conference Center in Albuquerque, NM. All members and interested persons are urged to attend. The keynote speaker is Dr. David Randol of the University of Edinburgh in Scotland.

About the IAA

Physician Referrals

Symptoms

Diagnosis

Treatment

Childhood Asthma

Publications

Research

Interesting Facts

Events

Membership

Email the IAA

The International Asthma Association presents

Asthma and You

Members log in **HERE**

Asthma is a chronic condition in which the lungs become inflamed and the airways narrow. The classic symptoms are shortness of breath, wheezing, and coughing. Sometimes there is chest pain and the neck muscles may tighten. Diagnosis is based on patient reports of what triggers the attacks and, sometimes, on skin and blood allergy tests.

This site has been designed with the patient in mind. Link to the newest research and discoveries about asthma. Find information on physicians in your area who specialize in allergies and asthma. Learn about ways to control asthma. Look for news about events.

The International Asthma Association is a not-for-profit foundation for the study and treatment of asthma. It was founded 20 years ago to research the causes and treatment of asthma. Dr. Beth Lee is director of this site. Email her at bethlee@iaa.org.

✏ Students click here!

Last updated: October, 2001

* URL is not real.

Plan

Once you've decided on your purpose, you're ready to begin examining the website. Use the strategy of reading critically.

• **Reading critically means examining the information you're given and deciding whether or not it is reliable.**

During Reading

Begin by reading the main menu. On this website, the menu runs along the left side of the site. Then let your eyes roam over the page.

D   Read with a Purpose

As you skim the web page, focus on finding answers to your purpose questions. Make notes on a Website Profiler. It can help you understand and evaluate elements of the website.

<u>Directions:</u> Read the website carefully and record your notes on this Website Profiler.

Website Profiler

Name	
URL	
Sponsor	**Date**
Point of View	**Expertise**
My Reaction	

Internet

Using the Strategy

Reading critically means examining the website carefully. Remember that not every link will be useful to your purpose. Use Study Cards to keep track of sites and information you want to remember.

• **When you read critically, you decide which links will be of help to meet your purpose.**

Directions: Make some notes about the International Asthma Association website on these Study Cards. What answers have you found to the questions on your K-W-L chart?

Study Cards

What are the symptoms of asthma?

My next question:

The answer:

Keep your Study Cards in front of you as you use the links on the site.

NAME ....

Understanding How Websites Are Organized

If you were to make a diagram of a website, you'd find that it really does look like a web. The "spokes" that reach out from the center of the web are paths or "links" that you can follow.

Directions: Complete this Web. List three important topics on the website.

Web

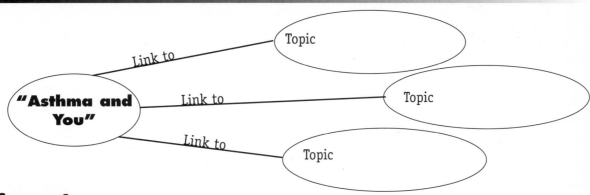

"Asthma and You"

Link to — Topic

Link to — Topic

Link to — Topic

 Connect

When you connect to a website, consider how you feel about the information. Does it anger you, surprise you, amuse you, or something else?

Directions: Think of two websites you've visited recently. Explain your opinion of each site and why you will or will not return.

Website #1

My opinion of it:

Why I will or will not return:

Website #2

My opinion of it:

Why I will or will not return:

Internet

After Reading

Take your time when doing research on the Internet. Gather your thoughts about one site before linking on to the next.

F Pause and Reflect

At this point, you'll want to recall your original purpose for visiting the site.

• **After you visit a website, ask yourself, "How well did I meet my purpose?"**

Directions: Return to the K-W-L Chart on page 186. Make some notes in the "L" column. Then explain what else you'd like to learn.

I need to find out more about _____ and _____

Links that might help _____

_____

_____

G Reread

Sometimes you may need to return to a site to double-check a fact or detail. Once again, think carefully about whether or not the information on the site is reliable.

• **A powerful rereading strategy to use when checking for reliability is skimming.**

Directions: Skim the website. Then answer the "reliability" questions on the organizer.

How to Evaluate Internet Success

1. What is the source of the site?	2. What credentials does the site offer?	3. What is the purpose of the site?
4. When was the site last updated?	5. Are there any obvious errors, misspellings, or typos?	

Remember

Good researchers remember what they've seen and learned.

• **Summary Notes can help you remember a website.**

Directions: Write a list of the four main things you learned at the "Asthma and You" website. Refer to your During Reading notes as needed.

Summary Notes

	website: http://www.iaa.asthma.com
●	Four things I learned at the asthma website: 1. 2. 3. 4.

Internet

Reading a Graphic

In a graphic, the words and visuals are equally important. Both contain vital information about the subject and purpose of the graphic.

Before Reading

Use the reading process and the strategy of paraphrasing to help you get more from a graphic.

A Set a Purpose

Your purpose for reading a graphic is to answer two general questions: "What is the graphic about?" and "What can it tell me?"

• **To set your purpose, ask two questions about the graphic.**

Directions: Write two purpose-setting questions for reading a graphic about the National Basketball Association (NBA) 2000–01 Finals. Then make a prediction.

Purpose question #1: ....

....

....

....

Purpose question #2: ....

....

....

....

My prediction: ....

....

....

NAME

B Preview the Reading

When you preview a graphic, look at both the words and the picture.

• **Pay attention to the title, all labels, and the visuals in a graphic.**

Directions: Preview the graphic below. Complete the Preview Notes.

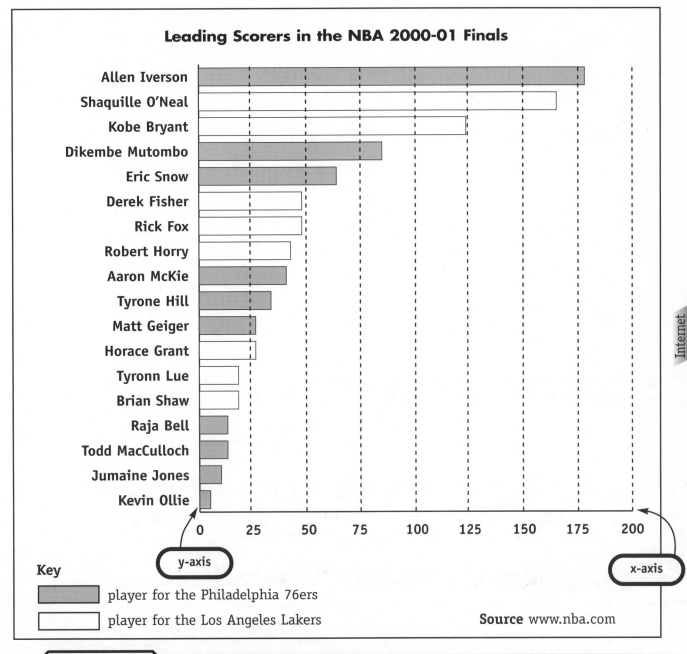

Leading Scorers in the NBA 2000-01 Finals

Source www.nba.com

Internet

◀ **Preview Notes**

The title: ....

The teams in the 2000–01 NBA Finals: ....
....

The source: ....

Plan

Your next step is to make a plan. Choose a strategy that will help you read and interpret the graphic.

> **• The strategy of paraphrasing can help you get more from a graphic.**

Put into your own words what the graphic shows.

During Reading

Now do a careful reading of the NBA Finals graphic. First look at the visual and decide what it shows. Then read the text.

 Read with a Purpose

Keep your purpose questions in mind as you read. Make notes about information that relates to these questions.

Directions: Read the "Leading Scorers" graphic. Then paraphrase, or tell in your own words, what the graphic shows.

What the graphic shows: ....

....

....

Using the Strategy

Putting information from another source in your own words is called *paraphrasing*. Paraphrasing can help you process information and remember what you've learned.

> **• Use a Paraphrase Chart to keep track of your ideas about the graphic.**

Directions: Complete the Paraphrase Chart. In addition to writing a paraphrase, record your thoughts about the graphic.

Paraphase Chart

Title	My Paraphrase

My Thoughts

Understanding How
Graphics Are Organized

Understanding the major parts of a graphic is key to unlocking what it says.

Directions: Label these elements on the graphic below: title, players, and points scored. Then answer the questions.

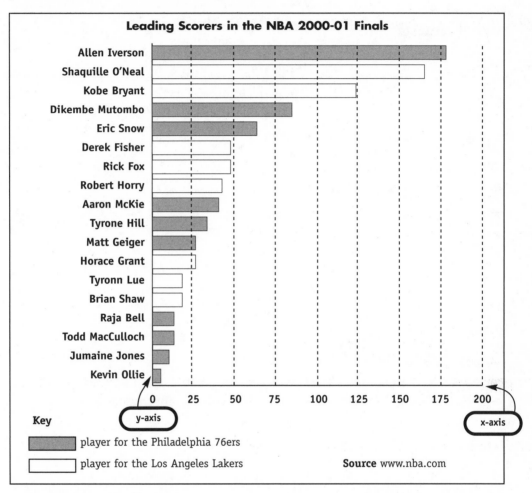

Leading Scorers in the NBA 2000-01 Finals

Key

■ player for the Philadelphia 76ers

□ player for the Los Angeles Lakers

Source www.nba.com

1. Which team had the top-scoring player?

....

2. What do Derek Fisher and Rick Fox have in common?

....

3. Which team had more high-scoring players? How do you know?

....

....

....

4. Whom would you predict won the 2000–01 Finals using this graph as evidence? Explain.

....

....

....

Connect

When you read a graphic, ask yourself, "What does this information mean to me?" On the left side of the chart, write a bit of information you learned. Then write your thoughts about that information on the right.

• **Use a Double-entry Journal to record your response to a graphic.**

Double-entry Journal

Information	My Thoughts

After Reading

After you finish paraphrasing and reacting to a graphic, take a second to look at it to make sure you haven't missed anything.

 Pause and Reflect

First, think back to your reading purpose. Decide whether you've answered both questions.

• **After you finish a selection, ask yourself, "How well did I meet my purpose?"**

<u>Directions:</u> Answer your reading purpose questions.

What is the graphic about?

....

....

What can it tell me?

....

....

NAME ....

 Reread

Look again at the NBA Finals graphic. Ask yourself, "What conclusions can I draw?"

• **Use the rereading strategy of reading critically to help you draw conclusions about a graphic.**

<u>Directions:</u> Complete this chart by looking again at the graphic critically.

◣ **Drawing Conclusions**

Questions to Ask	My Notes
What is being compared or classified in the graphic?	
Compare the data. What similarities and differences do you see?	
Think about what's not shown. Is there anything unusual about the way the data are presented? Is anything left out?	

H **Remember**

It's easier to remember a graphic if you *do* something with the information.

• **To remember a graphic, make a list of what you learned.**

<u>Directions:</u> Make a list of facts and details you learned from the graphic.

What I learned about the 2000-01 NBA Finals

1. ....

2. ....

3. ....

Internet

Reading a Test and Test Questions

Tests you take in school may be challenging, but they're never impossible. Here you'll learn a couple of strategies that can help you perform well on even the most difficult tests.

Before Reading

Of course, your *goal* when taking a test is to answer every question correctly. Use the reading process and the strategy of skimming to help you perform well when taking a test. So what is your reading purpose?

A Set a Purpose

Your purpose is to find out what the test questions are asking and decide what information is needed for the answers.

• **To set your purpose, ask a question about the test.**

Directions: For this sample test, you'll read a passage about the ballerina Maria Tallchief and then answer some test questions. Write your reading purpose here.

Purpose question: ....

....

....

B Preview

As soon as you receive a test, begin previewing. This will help you know what to expect.

Directions: Skim the sample test that follows. Read the directions and take a quick look at the questions. Use the preview stickies to make notes.

"America's Ballerina: Maria Tallchief"

English: Mid-year Reading Test

30 Minutes—5 questions, 1 essay

DIRECTIONS: Read each question. Choose the correct answer, and then circle the letter of the answer. Write your essay in the blue test booklet.

Mid-year Review, Passage #1

"America's Ballerina: Maria Tallchief"

What would it be like to be the premier dancer of a major ballet company? Think about this question as you read the article that follows.

America's Ballerina: Maria Tallchief

Maria Tallchief is known as the most technically accomplished American ballerina of all time. Her expressive movements, breathtaking poses, and gravity-defying leaps and lunges brought audiences to their feet in performance after performance. For more than thirty years, Tallchief danced to the music on the stage and the music in her heart. She is truly one of America's greatest performers of all time.

Betty Maria Tallchief was born in 1925 on an Osage Indian reservation in Oklahoma. Betty began dancing when she was a young child and quickly fell in love with all things ballet. When she was just seventeen, she joined the Ballet Russe de Monte Carlo. Shortly thereafter she dropped the name "Betty" and was introduced to audiences as Maria Tallchief, the newest star in the brightly lit world of ballet.

Over the next five years, word about Tallchief spread, and audiences stood in long lines for tickets to her performances. During this time, Tallchief was introduced to the brilliant choreographer George Balanchine. Balanchine was awed by Tallchief's talents and beauty. The two were married when Tallchief was 21 years old.

Inspired by Tallchief's "magic feet," Balanchine began creating roles for her that would showcase her amazing talent to audiences around the world. A year later, Tallchief left the Ballet Russe and together with Balanchine formed what would become the New York City Ballet (NYCB).

During her 18 years with NYCB, Tallchief held the position of *prima,* or premier, ballerina. Her performances in such ballets as *Orpheus, The Firebird, Swan Lake,* and *The Nutcracker* moved audiences to tears and brought worldwide fame to the ballet company. Critics who had said that America would never have a world-class ballet company were forced to eat their words.

What is the subject of the passage?

Tests

"America's Ballerina: Maria Tallchief," continued

Tallchief retired from dance in 1965, although she has since remained active in the ballet community. In 1953, the state of Oklahoma honored Tallchief for her achievements in the arts. She was given the name *Wa-Xthe-Thomba*, which means "Woman of Two Worlds." This name celebrates Tallchief's international achievements as a prima ballerina and Native American woman.

English: Mid-year Reading Test
Passage #1 Multiple-choice Questions
1. Maria Tallchief became famous for her . . .

    A. dancing   C. choreography

    B. Native American heritage   D. all of the above

2. Who founded the New York City Ballet?

    A. Balanchine   C. the Ballet Russe

    B. Tallchief   D. Balanchine and
                                           Tallchief together

3. What is a prima ballerina?

    A. a retired ballerina   C. a young ballerina

    B. a premier ballerina   D. an injured ballerina

4. Why do you suppose Tallchief retired from dance?

    A. She was tired of being injured.   C. She and Balanchine were

    B. She was getting too old to dance.   divorced.

                                       D. She had begun to hate dance.

5. What is the main idea of this article?

    A. Tallchief and Balanchine   C. Tallchief is the most technically
       were brilliant artists.   accomplished ballerina of all time.

    B. Tallchief overcame adversity   D. America finally has a world-class
       to become a prima ballerina.   ballet company.

Passage #1, Essay Question
6. Explain Tallchief's honorary name *Wa-Xthe-Thomba*. Discuss what it means and how she earned it. Use facts and details from the article to support your ideas.

Preview
Here's what I noticed about the questions:

Preview
Important information about the essay question:

Plan

Most tests have a combination of factual recall and critical thinking questions. What you need is a strategy that can help you answer both types of questions.

• **Use the strategy of skimming when you take tests.**

To answer most test questions, you'll need to return to the material and look for answers. This is why skimming is a good strategy to use.

During Reading

Read the entire passage carefully and then read the test questions.

Read with a Purpose

Use a highlighter to mark important sentences. Then mark important words in the test questions.

Directions: Read the passage on Maria Tallchief. Highlight or underline what you think are the most important sentences. Then summarize the passage in one or two sentences.

My summary: ....

....

....

Using the Strategy

Your next step will be to skim the passage for answers to the test questions.

• **When skimming, look for details that might relate to the author's main point.**

Directions: Read the five multiple-choice test questions on page 202. Tell where you should skim to find the answers.

Question #	Where I'll begin skimming—
1	As this is the first question, I should skim paragraph 1.
2	
3	
4	
5	

Tests

NAME ....

FOR USE WITH PAGES 564–579

Understanding How Tests Are Organized

Some of the tests you take will contain an essay question.
A graphic organizer can help you plan your essay.

Directions: Read the essay question on page 202.
Make notes on this organizer.

Main Idea Organizer

Topic: The honorary name Wa-Xthe-Thomba

Main Idea:

Detail #1	Detail #2	Detail #3

Concluding Sentence:

NAME

E Connect

As often as possible, make personal connections to a test passage as you read. Your comments can help you answer the essay questions.

- **Record your reactions to the person, place, or thing described in a test passage.**

Directions: Write three or more words that describe Maria Tallchief here. Try to think of words other than the ones used in the passage.

....

....

After Reading

After you complete a test, take a moment to gather your thoughts.

F Pause and Reflect

Ask yourself, "Have I answered each question to the best of my ability?"

- **After you finish a test, return to the questions that gave you the most trouble and double-check your answers.**

This is the multiple-choice question that I found most difficult: ....

....

Here's why: ....

....

....

Here's how the strategy of skimming helped me answer the question: ....

....

....

....

....

Tests

Reread

When you finish the easiest questions on the test, return to the more challenging ones. These are often inference or conclusion questions.

• **Read at least three sentences to answer each question.**

Directions: Read this inference question. Then write a Think Aloud that tells how you figured out the answer.

---

4. Why do you suppose Tallchief retired from dance?
   A. She was tired of being injured.   C. She and Balanchine were divorced.
   B. She was getting too old to dance.   D. She had begun to hate dance.

◄ Think Aloud

....

....

....

....

 Remember

Take a careful look at a test after your teacher has graded it. Figure out what you did wrong and avoid making the same mistake on future tests.

• **Remember the test questions that gave you trouble.**

Directions: Exchange books with a classmate. "Grade" each other's tests, and comment on the Think Alouds. Then write what *you* can do to improve your test-taking abilities.

I can improve my test-taking abilities by ....

....

....

....

Focus on Essay Tests

Essay tests are not as hard as you think. What you need is a plan that you can follow as you're taking the test.

Step 1: Preview and read carefully.

First, preview the directions and writing prompt, and then make notes about what the question is asking.

Directions: Read the essay assignment and prompt. Underline key words and phrases. Then note at least three things you have to do.

DIRECTIONS: Write an opinion essay about a proposed school board rule. First read the prompt below. Then write your opinion statement. Next offer support for your opinion. Carefully proofread your writing when you're done.

  Prompt: Your school board is proposing a rule to ban cell phones and beepers on school property. How do you feel about this proposal? Write an essay stating your opinion. Support it with convincing evidence.

---

1. First

What I need to do to write this essay:

2. Then

3. After that

Tests

Step 2: Organize.

Take the time to organize your essay before you begin writing.

Directions: Use this Main Idea Organizer to plan your essay.

Main Idea Organizer

Your Opinion:		
Supporting Detail 1	**Supporting Detail 2**	**Supporting Detail 3**

Concluding Sentence:

NAME ....

FOR USE WITH PAGES 580–583

Step 3: Write.

Refer to your Main Idea Organizer as you write. In your introduction, state your opinion. In the body of the essay, offer your support.

Directions: Write the your essay here.

....

....

....

....

....

....

....

....

....

....

....

....

....

....

....

....

Step 4: Proofread.

Failure to proofread can affect your score. Check for problems with spelling, mechanics, and usage.

Directions: Proofread the essay you wrote. Make corrections neatly.

Tests

Focus on Vocabulary Tests

To score well on a vocabulary test, you must have a strong knowledge of words and word parts. You also need to understand the relationship between words in an analogy. Follow these steps.

Step 1: Preview.

Begin by skimming the test to see what type of questions you'll be expected to answer. Then highlight any vocabulary terms, such as *synonym, antonym,* or *analogy.*

Directions: Preview these sample test questions. Highlight any vocabulary terms.

Sample Test Questions

Directions: Find the synonym for each underlined word.

1. The willowy girl was as <u>slender</u> as a reed.

   A. plump   B. strong   C. thin   D. fragile

2. I am <u>confident</u> that I will win the talent show contest.

   A. certain   B. predicting   C. uncertain   D. happy

Step 2: Eliminate wrong answers.

Read every choice, even if you're sure you know the right one. Then eliminate answers that are clearly *wrong*.

Directions: Look at the questions again. Cross out the answers you know are wrong.

Step 3: Use context clues.

Next, check the words near the unknown word. Look for clues about the unknown word's meaning.

Directions: Reread the questions. What context clues do you find for the word *slender?* What context clues do you find for *confident?*

Context Clue #1:   What it tells me:
....

....

Context Clue #2:   What it tells me:

....

Step 4: Figure out word relationships.

To solve an analogy, first figure out how the word pair is related. Then choose another pair that has the same relationship.

Directions: First, review the section on word analogies in your handbook. Then tell the relationship between the words *rage* and *anger.* Finish by solving the analogy.

---

rage : anger ::

A. found : lose   C. cure : heal

B. test : student   D. animal : cat

How rage and anger are related:
....

The correct answer is   because
....

....

Step 5: Check.

Save a few minutes at the end of the test to check your work.

Directions: Answer the sample questions. Then compare your answers with those of a classmate. If you disagree, talk through the questions and answers.

Focus on Social Studies Tests

To do well on a social studies test, you must know names and places, dates and events, and big ideas in history. You also must read very carefully. Follow these steps to improve your score.

Step 1: Preview.

Quickly skim the test directions and questions. Use a highlighter to mark topics you're familiar with. Answer the "easy" questions first.

Directions: Take a quick look at the sample questions. Highlight all important words.

Sample Test Questions

DIRECTIONS: Fill in the circle next to the correct answer.

1. In what country did the Industrial Revolution begin in the 1760s?

   ○ A. England   ○ C. the United States

   ○ B. Europe   ○ D. Russia

2. What was the pattern of migration during the Industrial Revolution?

   ○ A. from coastal to inland areas

   ○ B. from cities to suburbs

   ○ C. from rural to urban areas

   ○ D. from urban to rural areas

Step 2: Rule out wrong answers.

Next, look for answers you know are *wrong*.

Directions: Return to the first test question. Cross out the answers you know are wrong. (Hint: Keep in mind the date the Revolution began. Remember also that you are looking for a *country* name.)

Step 3: Reread the question.

Reread the question until you're sure you know what it's asking.

Directions: Tell what Question 1 is asking you to figure out.

Question 1 wants me to figure out ....

....

....

Step 4: Talk your way through the possible answers.

Quietly think aloud about the remaining answers to the question.

Directions: Complete this Think Aloud for Question 1.

Think Aloud

I know that B is wrong because Europe is not a country. It is a continent.

I also think _____ might be wrong because ....

....

....

Step 5: Choose an answer and double-check.

Finally, make your choice. Then reread the question to see if the answer you've chosen makes sense.

Directions: Write what you think is the correct answer to Question 1. Then explain your choice.

My answer: ....

....

....

My explanation: ....

....

....

....

Tests

Focus on Math Tests

Math tests require careful attention. You'll need to call on everything you know. Follow these steps to improve your score.

Step 1: Preview.

Always begin by previewing the test. Look for the most important information in each question.

Directions: Preview the sample questions. Highlight the most important parts.

Sample Test Questions

1. A small pizza at Villa Rosa costs $6.50. A large soda costs $1.75. You bring a roll of 40 quarters to Villa Rosa to pay for a pizza and soda. How many quarters will you need to use to pay for the meal?

   A. 40   C. 33

   B. 34   D. 26

2. You are treating yourself and each of three friends to a hamburger and soft drink. A hamburger at Sam's Diner costs $2.40. A large soft drink costs $1.50. You have two rolls of 40 quarters each. How many quarters will you need to use?

   A. 83   C. 47

   B. 36   D. 63

Step 2: Eliminate.

Whenever possible, use number sense to eliminate answers that are clearly *wrong*.

Directions: Return to the sample questions. Cross out the answers that are clearly wrong. (Hint: For Question 1, one of the answers is too high and another is too low.)

Step 3: Estimate.

Always estimate the answer if you can. Doing some rough calculations may help you rule out one or more answers.

Directions: Look at Question 1 again. Then estimate how much the meal will cost.

I estimate that the meal will cost ....

....

Step 4: Visualize.

Try to visualize what the problem is saying. This can make it easier to understand and solve.

Directions: Make a sketch that reflects Question 1.

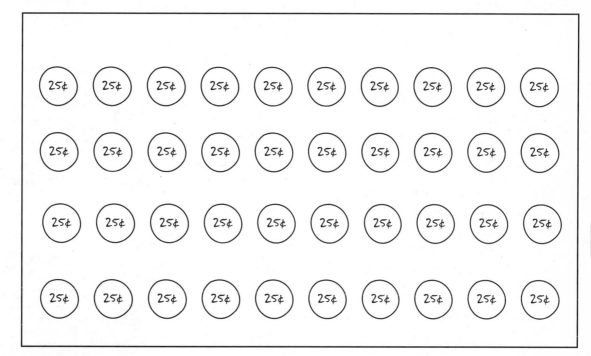

Step 5: Check.

To check your work, use a *different* method to solve the same problem.

Directions: Rewrite Question 1 as an equation. Write one equation to figure out the cost of the meal and another to figure out how many quarters are needed to pay for the meal.

Meal cost equation: ....

Quarters needed equation: ....

Focus on Science Tests

To succeed on a science test, you need to think like a scientist. Follow these steps.

Step 1: Prepare for the test.

Review your notes. Skim for key terms and their definitions. Look again at any graphics in the text.

Directions: Read the paragraph and diagram. Mark scientific terms. Write notes.

Sample Test Items

The Earth's Crust

Scientists estimate that the earth formed from a cloud of dust particles approximately 4.6 billion years ago. The dust particles joined together to create a ball of molten, or melted, rock. Eventually the ball cooled and formed a crust on the outside. This crust is the surface of the earth.

Planet Earth

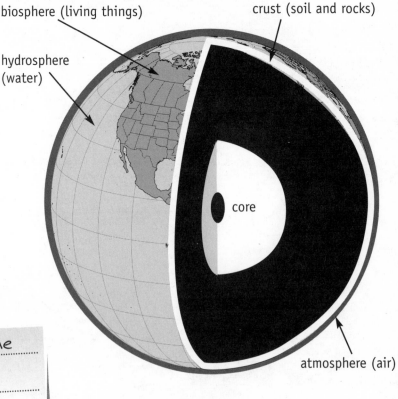

biosphere (living things)

crust (soil and rocks)

hydrosphere (water)

core

atmosphere (air)

Important information in the reading

_____

_____

_____

_____

This diagram shows

_____

_____

_____

_____

Step 2: Preview the test.

On the day of the test, read the directions, questions, and graphics quickly to get an idea of what they are about.

Directions: Preview the questions. Explain what you need to find out.

Sample Questions

> 1. Which came first, dust particles or molten rock?
>
> 2. What is at the center of the Earth?

For Question 1, I need to find out

....

....:

For Question 2, I need to find out

....

....:

Step 3: Think aloud.

Talk your way through possible answers to the questions.

Directions: Complete this Think Aloud for the two questions in Step 2.

Think Aloud

For Question 1, I'll look at the reading and
....

For Question 2, I'll look at the diagram and
....

Step 4: Check.

Check your answers by rewriting the questions as statements.

Directions: Rewrite the questions. Check that each statement is true.

Question 1 rewritten as a statement:
....

....

Question 2 rewritten as a statement:
....

....

Tests

Learning New Words

Words help you understand, connect ideas, and express new ideas as you write and talk about your thoughts and feelings. It makes sense, then, to learn as many new words as you can. Follow these steps to build your vocabulary.

Step 1: Read.

When you come to an unfamiliar word in your reading, don't just skip it—"collect" it. Take time to learn what the word means.

Directions: Read this passage. Circle words that are unfamiliar to you.

> **from *Jacob Have I Loved* by Katherine Paterson**
>
> During the summer of 1941, every weekday morning at the top of the tide, McCall Purnell and I would board my skiff and go progging for crab. Call and I were right smart crabbers, and we could always come home with a little money as well as plenty of crab for supper. Call was a year older than I and would never have gone crabbing with a girl except that his father was dead, so he had no man to take him on board a regular crab boat. He was, as well, a boy who had matured slowly, and being fat and nearsighted, he was dismissed by most of the island boys.
>
> Call and I made quite a pair. At thirteen I was tall and large boned, with delusions of beauty and romance. He, at fourteen, was pudgy, bespectacled, and totally unsentimental.

Step 2: Record.

In your reading journal, keep a list of unfamiliar words. Add to the list each time you read. Be sure to note where you found the words.

NAME FOR USE WITH PAGES 608–614

Directions: Write the words you circled on this journal page. You'll define them later.

Student Journal

English

from Jacob Have I Loved

Unfamiliar Words	Definitions

Step 3: Define.

Next, use a dictionary to define the words on your list. Choose the definition that matches the way the word is used in the book.

Directions: Get together with a partner. Work with your partner to define the words on your list. Write the definitions on the chart above.

Step 4: Use.

The best way to remember a new word is to use it in conversation or in writing.

Directions: Working with your partner, write one sentence for each of the words you defined.

My Sentences

1. ______
2. ______
3. ______
4. ______

Vocabulary

Building Vocabulary Skills

You can build your vocabulary by learning the technique of defining in context and by learning some basic word families. Practice here.

Step 1: Use context clues.

You won't always be able to use a dictionary to find the meaning of an unfamiliar word. If no dictionary is available, context clues can help.

Directions: Review pages 615–620 in your handbook. Then read this excerpt. Use context clues to figure out the meaning of the underlined words. Make notes on the chart. We've done one for you.

from *Bury My Heart at Wounded Knee* by Dee Brown

"So <u>tractable</u>, so peaceable, are these people," Columbus wrote to the King and Queen of Spain, "that I swear to your Majesties that there is not in the world a better nation. They love their neighbors as themselves, and their <u>discourse</u> is ever sweet and gentle, and accompanied with a smile; and though it is true that they are naked, yet their manners are <u>decorous</u> and praiseworthy."

Context Clues Chart

Underlined Words	My Definition	Context Clues I Used
tractable	easy to deal with	I see the word <u>peaceful</u> and his comment that they are a wonderful nation.

Step 2: Use word parts.

Knowing various word parts, such as prefixes, suffixes, and roots, can help you increase the number of new words you can understand.

Roots

Directions: Complete this word tree. Add words that have the root *form*.

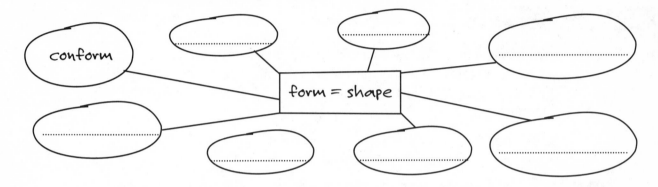

Prefixes

dis- = not, opposite	*anti-* = against	*pre-* = before

Directions: Add a prefix to each word. Write the meaning.

Prefix	+	Word =	New Word	Meaning of New Word
1.		+ content		
2.		+ freeze		
3.		+ view		

Suffixes

-en = to make	*-ence* = state or quality of	*-age* = action or progress

Directions: Add a suffix from the box to these words. Then use each word in a sentence.

strength + -en = ...

differ + -ence = ...

pilgrim + -age = ...

Vocabulary

Dictionary Dipping

A dictionary is an indispensable tool for readers. Learn how to get more from every dictionary entry you read.

Step 1: Read the entry.

Usually when you pick up a dictionary, you do so because you need to know the meaning or pronunciation of a specific word. Once you've found the entry you're looking for, read the word's definition carefully and make some notes.

Directions: Read the definition for *temperate*. Then answer these questions. Review page 629 in your handbook if you get stuck.

Dictionary Entry

temperate (tem´ pər it) *adj.* **1.** not very hot and not very cold. **2.** using self-control; moderate: *She spoke in a temperate manner and did not favor one side over another.* [from the Latin *temperare*, which originally meant "observe in a careful way"] —*adv.* **temperately.**

1. How many definitions does *temperate* have? ....

2. What part of speech is *temperate?* ....

3. What is the history of the word? ....

Step 2: Remember.

The easiest way to remember a new word is to use it.

Directions: Write two sentences for the word *temperate*.

Sentence #1: ....

....

Sentence #2: ....

....

Reading a  Thesaurus

A thesaurus is like a treasure chest of words. Unlocking the chest can be as simple as reading carefully.

Step 1: Read the entry.

When you pick up a thesaurus, you do so with a specific purpose in mind—to find synonyms for a given word. Begin by searching for an entry for the given word. Then read the synonyms listed.

Directions: Read the entry for *disloyal*. Then answer these questions. Review page 630 in your handbook if you need help.

Thesaurus Entry

> **disloyal** *adjective* **1. betraying, faithless, false, untrustworthy** Ana is never disloyal to her friends. **2. traitorous, treacherous** Acting as a spy is disloyal. **3. cheating, double-crossing** One partner accused the other of being a disloyal thief.**—*Antonyms:* faithful, loyal, true.

1. What part of speech is *disloyal?* _____

2. What are some synonyms for *disloyal?* _____

3. What are some antonyms? _____

Step 2: Use the synonyms.

To help you remember the synonyms you found, practice using them.

Directions: Complete these sentences using synonyms for *disloyal*.

The leaders of the American Revolution were thought by England to be

disloyal to their ruler. The patriots didn't see the situation in the same way.

How could it be _____ to want to govern themselves? When they

were accused of being _____ , they protested and eventually went

to war.

Author/Title Index

Acknowledgements

15 From THE LATIN DELI: PROSE AND POETRY by Judith Ortiz Cofer. © 1993 by Judith Ortiz Cofer. All rights reserved.

Photo Credits

20 courtesy Library of Congress

21 courtesy Library of Congress

39 ©Photodisc

81 ©Corbis

94 ©Bettman/Corbis

102 ©Corbis